THERIACA ELIXIR

a botanical formula for the 21st century
for vitality and well being

THE BOOKLET

by Tony & Sylvia Samara

for

Title: Theriaca Elixir – a botanical formula for the 21st century – for vitality and well being – The Booklet

Authors: Tony Samara & Sylvia Samara

First Edition - November 2010

Disclaimer: The statements in this book have not been evaluated by any Health Authorities in any country. Theriaca Elixir is not a substitute for a medical exam. Any reference to medicinal properties or health is not meant to treat or diagnose any problem nor is it meant to replace professional medical advice. Theriaca Elixir should not take the place of any medication that has been prescribed by a physician.

Table of Contents

FOREWORD

As a spiritual guide, I work with many people through a very powerful initiation process and this is sometimes very, very strong. I noticed that during these intense times, the body could not cope with the changes, as if the body would stay behind even though every other aspect of the person was receiving light, the body was still there, holding the person back with its processes and dynamics. I was particularly struck by this because a few people that have been working with me for many years were still experiencing this persisting weight. I know of nothing more powerful than this initiation work that I do and still the body was like a solid rock. It was too heavy and not changing enough.

When I realised this, I worked during a special night to create the formula that is now called Theriaca Elixir. This formula has evolved since that night, but it was the base of what you are drinking today.

In this book, it is explained that Theriaca Elixir is for helping to heal cancer and many other things. Even though Theriaca Elixir is amazing in the physical realm, the reason why I created it was for another type of healing: to heal the DNA structure of the person.

How is this done? Some of the plants that I have used are unknown to most people but they are very well known in the places that they come from. No one is exactly sure how they work. Some of them are the most powerful natural antioxidants known to man. They are not synthetic so they remove what is preventing light from coming into your cells and into the structure of your physical being. That is one of the scientific aspects of it, which is interesting but it is not the whole story.

One of the plants is a little mushroom that grows wild in the forests of Brazil and it has been used by the native people in the forest for thousands of years. It has only recently been discovered because a Japanese scientist went there and was amazed that it worked to heal cancer in a real scientific sense where they used tests, graphs and statistics. But the native people aren't scientists.

If you go to Brazil, there are thousands of mushrooms growing everywhere. It is very humid and it is a wonderful place for mushrooms to grow. How did they find out that this specific mushroom, out of the hundreds of varieties that grow in the forest, was a very healing one? They don't have a lab to test anything…

It is very easy. They go into the forest and they close their eyes. They look around with their eyes closed and then they walk towards whatever is shining bright, with an immense light. If you can see this, when you walk towards this mushroom, its light is immense. It is so strong that when you put this light into your body, it starts to penetrate into the DNA structure. I do not know how to explain this scientifically or medically, but it helps the DNA structure to become this light. This is the light that is universal and that I believe is expanding now much stronger than ever.

It is almost as if parts inside of you were being tuned like a piano. The ingredients of Theriaca Elixir are the pure tunes that are going into your body so that you can receive the melodies, the sounds and the light of the universe. This is what I believe is very important and this is the main reason why I created Theriaca Elixir.

It is the most wonderful way to nourish yourself, to open up any walls inside of you and to step out into a space where it is good to be receptive and receive the healing light from nature.

Tony Samara

THERIACA ELIXIR

A BOTANICAL FORMULA FOR THE 21ST CENTURY
FOR VITALITY AND WELL BEING

Theriaca Elixir can play a vital role as an antidote to our modern lifestyles, environmental pollution, stresses and imbalances of energy.

Many ancient cultures drank healing herbal teas knowing that the adaptogenic, cleansing and rejuvenating tonic ingredients were vital for good health. Rediscover this ancient healing form and empower body, mind and spirit. As scientists are today discovering, a clear flow of energy enables graceful, harmonious and vigourous living.

The unique characteristic of Theriaca Elixir lies in its masterful combining of ingredients by Tony Samara, creating an enhanced, synergistic effect. This means that drinking Theriaca Elixir has a far greater effect than does the taking of each ingredient separately.

An infusion of Theriaca Elixir creates a strong, fragrant, full-bodied yet smooth and lively tasting brew that can be drunk several times daily. Historically the ingredients are recognised for their outstanding medicinal virtues, due to their high nutritional value and mineral content, and are widely used among people renowned for their longevity.

Theriaca Elixir contains only organic ingredients of the highest quality from producers who have implemented organic growing methods combined with outstanding standards of social and economic welfare. Some of the ingredients can only be found in nature and are hence wild-crafted; selected solely from pristine natural environments. This ensures the protection of the land, the people that live and work on it and the wildlife found there, sustaining a balanced fertile and naturally harmonious environment.

Theriaca Elixir is naturally alkalinising and extremely high in anti-oxidants, saponins, germanium, resveratrol, beta-glucans and a full spectrum of rare health-enhancing nutrients and minerals.

I. THE ELIXIR

Natural nutritional supplementation is no longer just a good idea —in today's world it is essential to maintain health and vitality. But with the vast array of supplements and herbal tea products on the market today, how do you choose which nutrients your body really needs?

Excellent nutrition has never been simpler and Tony Samara will now explain the importance of Theriaca Elixir in our everyday life.

Tony Samara says, "In today's world, nutrition is vital. We may get occasional and life-sustaining nutrients from our everyday diet but to catch up and keep up with today's extraordinary demands we must seek out essential nutrients and minerals to flood our systems so that our health is not only optimal but our well-being is functioning at its peak.

This entails eating fresh and natural foods such as vegetables, fruits, grains, and nutrient dense herbs such as Theriaca Elixir that cleanse and supplement and super-charge the whole process of living that is missing in today's modern society.

The Weston A. Price Foundation speaks about the vitamins and nutrients present in fresh food becoming more optimum in the presence of certain naturally occurring co-factors such as trace minerals and vitamins. These trace minerals, vitamins and co-factors are abundantly present in Theriaca Elixir and are what give this product its tremendous life-giving synergy.

Part of what makes Theriaca Elixir an essential part of our daily routine is its supply of an incredible depth and breadth of critical anti-oxidants like superoxide dismutase (SOD) and a host of other key micro-nutrients including saponins which have been found to support the immune system in an incredible and remarkable way.

All of the ingredients have centuries of tradition and are supported by impressive research and today are being discovered as wonder nutrients by the scientific community.

The unique ingredients have powerful anti-ageing, anti-viral, anti-fungal, anti-parasitic, antiseptic, anti-bacterial, anti-tumour as well anti-oxidant properties of awesome proportions. Studies of these compounds confirm that they protect, heal and even reverse modern day sicknesses. These powerful ingredients revitalise the body's most fragile tissues preventing abnormal cell growth. They help stop oxidation, inflammation and the damaging cycle of disease before it starts.

Historically mankind used herbs as a powerful means to protect and enhance health and well-being helping to create longevity, rejuvenation and a sense of extraordinary well-being that helps us today to re-experience these extraordinary health benefits.

Theriaca Elixir is a powerful nutritive energiser and cleanser. It works gently yet when taken for 2 or 3 months creates an amazing balance that is sensed not only on the physical level but also in the mind and the emotions. This balance is due to its synergistic and adaptogenic effects.

Modern society has shown an increase in many physiological and psychological problems such as insomnia, irritability, lack of energy as well as cancer, heart problems, diabetes and immune disorder.

The good news is that today we know that many rare essential minerals and nutrients can reverse and prevent what has become a major issue for many of us despite modern advances in medicine."

II. DRINKING THERIACA ELIXIR

To appreciate Theriaca at its best, pour one litre of filtered, spring or bottled boiled water into a teapot and leave it to cool down for about 30 seconds. Place one heaped dessert spoon (approx 2g) of Theriaca into the teapot. Leave this to brew for at least 3-5 minutes. Sip slowly and savour the flavour whilst enjoying a refreshing pick-me-up experience with powerful health benefits.

We also suggest you use a glass teapot that has a tea strainer inside for your Theriaca preparation, even though any teapot will work of course. This allows you to brew Theriaca in an optimum way so that all the properties can become more alive and powerful. Using this kind of teapot please consider leaving the ingredients to brew longer than the suggested 3-5 minutes so that the Theriaca can form a smoother, tastier and stronger experience.

The instructions on the Theriaca Elixir label are guidelines and are not meant to be dogmatic rules. For example, if one sips the elixir after it has brewed for more than 5 minutes, Theriaca Elixir just gets stronger so it is better. We leave our pot standing all day and drink it little by little. Another example is that the 1 litre quantity that is mentioned on the label as a recommended daily dose is for when you require a strongly healing dose otherwise 1 or 2 glasses a day is sufficient.

People with cancer, Alzheimer's disease, multiple sclerosis, advanced arthritis, chronic heart disease and any other disease can all highly benefit from drinking Theriaca Elixir, as one will understand by reading the descriptions of the ingredients in this booklet. The word elixir is the key, Theriaca Elixir is able to support the healing of everything and there are no contraindications or known interactions with any drugs so even if you are undergoing medical treatment, you can assist this process by drinking Theriaca Elixir daily and it is even beneficial during pregnancy. However, Tony Samara recommends that no more than 3 cups a day should be sipped when pregnant.

An important point is that one Theriaca Elixir batch is meant for only one brew. It is usually better to put the appropriate amount into a teapot if you want more than one cup because the benefit is lost if you reuse the same batch of Theriaca Elixir several times. If this happens you may introduce unwanted bacteria because it is not just a tea but has many food substances in it, which is part of what makes it such an essential elixir.

The mushrooms in Theriaca Elixir are medicinal mushrooms in a dry form (rather than fresh food mushrooms) that have been shown to be very beneficial with Candida problems as well as other serious diseases. Tony Samara recommends these as well as a healthy diet as a means of improving the ecology of the body so that Candida is no longer a problem because Candida is much more common than we think. Many of the herbs utilised encourage the regrowth of friendly bacteria so that Candida is eliminated. The formula is synergistically combined to eliminate the environment that creates disease.

If weight loss is of interest, Theriaca Elixir can also assist with this. One wonderful way to use it is with a mono diet. A mono diet means eating only fruit, or eating only one type of vegetable or grain for a few days and drinking the elixir to help with the detoxifying process.

Theriaca Elixir of course also helps when we feel depressed, emotionally depleted or overwhelmed by everyday life. Tony Samara believes that Theriaca Elixir is not simply beneficial in a physical way but very importantly helps the body organs, glands, and cells to function more harmoniously. This has the same effect on mind, body and spirit thus giving many of us who drink Theriaca Elixir on a regular basis, a sense of inner well-being. Tony Samara believes Theriaca Elixir to be vital as we prepare for the many changes happening in our world today, which strongly affect us in many more ways than just on a physical level. Theriaca Elixir contains many trace minerals that help with the transformational process that happens as we cleanse our bodies, freeing the mind and emotions to discover joy and a sense of lightness.

Animals can also benefit from Theriaca Elixir, one of our distributors has reported that her cat, which has leukaemia, naturally started to eat all the remains of Theriaca Elixir that she had put aside on a plate. The following day she brewed some Theriaca Elixir specifically for the cat and it drank all the tea faster than it would drink her usual liquids indicating a natural instinct and understanding from the animal that Theriaca Elixir is beneficial for all beings.

One distributor has asked:

"I get many people interested in Theriaca Elixir but they say they don't usually drink tea and that it's just not part of their eating habits. I was wondering what to do to make them benefit from Theriaca Elixir anyway, without having to drink it. I thought to use it in the preparation of food, like a seasoning that can be used either raw in salads or cooked in prepared dishes. If used in this way, will the properties of Theriaca Elixir still be kept intact? Would it have the same healing properties?"

Here is the reply from Tony Samara.

"We already have suggested to some people that the remains of Theriaca Elixir after brewing and drinking can be added to food and we have done this on various occasions ourselves.

As for drinking tea I am not so into this either and instead I brew in the morning for one hot/warm cup and drink it cold in the afternoon. Sometimes I even add fruit juice - organic red grape juice is my favourite."

The distributor continues, "I have just prepared a stir fry and added Theriaca Elixir with a bit of turmeric. It tastes great!"

Tony's comment, "Stir fry is a great idea!"

Another distributor has asked:

"Is Theriaca Elixir raw? Can I use it in my Raw Food Centre?"

The answer is that yes, "Everything in Theriaca Elixir is 100% raw, organic or wild-crafted.

All the items have been selected from pristine environments and preserved in a way that doesn't detract from the plant's natural goodness.

Nothing has been heated, irradiated or preserved in any of the ways that modern foodstuffs are often subjected to. The packaging is also totally ecological.

The water for Theriaca Elixir is normally boiled to make a tea but you can heat it to 45 degrees or place it outside in the sun in a glass jar and this will create an infusion. Alternatively it can be ground and sprinkled as an amazing healing herb on top of salads and in smoothies.

This is a product that you will understand by using.

You will find that a lot of its properties are adaptogenic meaning that they become obvious over time as they work with different parts of your body, physically and emotionally."

III. WHO IS TONY SAMARA?

After living for several years in a Zen Buddhist monastery, Tony Samara ventured to the jungles of South America - to the Amazon and to the Andes - where he lived and studied among a community of Shamans. After many years he was initiated in the sacred healing ways of these ancient peoples and left South America to teach and share this deep wisdom with the world.

Tony Samara is now visited by people from all parts of the world and from all walks of life, seeking spiritual guidance or simply the experience of being in his presence. He is a mirror of what is possible, a shining reminder of the endless potential of being human.

Like many spiritual teachers, Tony Samara is concerned with practical inner work and liberation. He teaches by personal example and instruction, guiding the seeker to realise bliss here and now, through growing spiritual awareness rather than mental effort.

Part of Tony Samara's teachings remind us that food and eating are fundamental to our inner well being, as well as to our physical health. He explains in his many programmes that the body is our temple and that the food we eat helps us to create a strong foundation that allows inner work and transformation to take place. He also explains that food is not just a physical substance which nourishes the body but that it also contains spiritual and emotional energy. Hence the importance of being conscious and taking the time to be present when we are eating and to become more sensitive to what will nourish our body, our temple rather than eat only what we feel like eating.

Tony Samara also encourages a balanced vegetarian diet, which includes organic products that are full of life force.

IV. THE LIFE ENHANCING PROPERTIES OF THERIACA ELIXIR

According to Tony Samara, Theriaca Elixir has the ultimate curing and healing capacity for every aspect of disease.

To explain more:

It is an anti-oxidant so it assists in removing many toxins from the body.

It is an alkalinising elixir, which means that it changes the chemistry of the body to change the physical environment to a healing one.

It is an adaptogen which means the more you drink the stronger the effect the healing by boosting organs, energy levels, hormone balance and a sense of mental well-being.

It contains virtually all the beneficial minerals known to man so it replaces trace minerals that are very much missing in the modern diet.

It has substances similar to antibiotics, which help to heal the body from parasites and viruses.

It contains saponins which are immune stimulants that are especially useful in times of low energy and disease.

It also contains germanium and Pau d'Arco, which oxygenate the body and are especially useful if you smoke, live in polluted cities or don't exercise.

It contains beta-glucans which are amazingly healing for weak bodies.

Theriaca Elixir also contains ingredients that are not fully researched but have been shown in native societies to create an amazing sense of health and freedom from disease, extending life so that people are very long-lived without losing mental or physical faculties.

And of course, Theriaca Elixir contains Tony Samara's alchemical magic.

The mixture is in a very specific proportion that makes it much more than the ingredients as they synergistically work together. A little bit similar to an ancient formula called ESSIAC formula, but much more relevant in today's world.

V. THERIACA ELIXIR'S INGREDIENTS

1) **Jiaogulan** (*Gynostemma pentaphyllum*)

Gynostemma pentaphyllum, also called Jiaogulan is an herbaceous vine of the family Cucurbitaceae (cucumber or gourd family) indigenous to the southern reaches of China, southern Korea and Japan. Jiaogulan is best known as a herbal medicine reputed to have powerful antioxidant and adaptogenic effects that increase longevity.

Jiaogulan leaves

History

The 1970 population census in China revealed that in the provinces of Guangxi and Shicuan, in southern China many people lived past the age of 100. The Chinese government wanted to know why and commissioned a team of researchers from the Chinese Academy of Medical Sciences to investigate. The researchers considered genetics, climate, diet and many other factors. The researchers reported in popular daily newspapers that many local consumed a tea made from a local wild vine. In fact, the locals gave the researchers a big clue. They called this plant "Xiancao", the immortality herb. Researchers identified the plant as Jiaogulan (known in latin as Gynostemma pentaphyllum).

The plant is best known for its use as an herbal medicine in traditional Chinese medicine, although its inclusion in Wu Qi-Jun's 1848 botany book Zhi Wu Ming Shi Tu Kao Chang Bian discusses a few medicinal uses and seems to be the earliest known documentation of the herb. Prior to that, Jiaogulan was cited as a survival food in Zu Xio's 1406 book Materia Medica for Famine. Until recently it was a locally known herb used primarily in regions of southern China. Most research has been done since the Chinese realised that it might be an inexpensive source for adaptogenic compounds, taking pressure off of ginseng stock.

Medicinal uses and scientific research

Although it has been used to treat a wide range of diseases in its native areas of China, gynostemma has been studied most for its effects on the cardiovascular system (the heart and blood vessels). Gynostemma may have a direct strengthening effect on the heart, possibly causing the heart to beat more powerfully. It may also have a number of secondary cardiovascular effects, such as reducing the stickiness of blood components called platelets. Created in the bone marrow, platelets circulate in the blood. In a process called "platelet aggregation", they stick to injured tissue, beginning the blood clotting process and promoting wound healing. Gynostemma's potential reduction in platelet aggregation may help to reduce the build up of plaques in blood vessels. Plaques are accumulations of fats and blood cells that may lead to heart attacks or strokes if blood flow becomes restricted. In addition, gynostemma has been shown in laboratory studies to widen blood vessels--an effect that may both lower blood pressure and reduce the workload on the heart. Some evidence suggests that gynostemma also contains chemicals that may lower cholesterol levels in the blood.

Because it is an antioxidant, gynostemma may also have potential as an anticancer and immune-stimulating agent. Antioxidants are thought to protect body cells from damage caused by a chemical process called oxidation, which produces oxygen free radicals, natural chemicals that may also suppress immune function. As shown in laboratory studies of human cancer cells, gynostemma may disrupt normal cell division in cancer cells, thereby preventing or delaying the onset of cancer and possibly destroying existing cancerous tumours. This anticancer effect has also been seen in early results from a few animal studies. Separate animal studies show that gynostemma may also help to regulate the immune system-- possibly by stimulating B cells and T cells. When it was given to animals with either deficient or overactive immune systems, gynostemma appeared to return immune function to levels that are more normal.

The antioxidant effects of gynostemma may also protect the liver from some of the damage caused by certain drugs or chemicals or by chronic alcohol abuse. In animal studies, gynostemma has interfered with the development of liver fibrosis-- the formation of scar-like fibres in the liver. Because the non-functioning fibers crowd out active liver tissue, liver function decreases gradually as the amount of fibrous tissue increases.

It is known as an adaptogen and antioxidant and has been found to increase superoxide dismutase (SOD) which is a powerful endogenous cellular antioxidant, one of the body's most important, and studies show that charting SOD levels in various animal species is a reliable indicator of their longevity. Trials in humans showed that SOD levels may return to youthful levels after taking 20 mg of Gypenosides (active elements in Jiaogulan) daily for one month. Studies have found that Jiaogulan increases the activities of macrophages, T lymphocytes and natural killer cells and that it acts as a tumour inhibitor.

Due to its adaptogenic effects it is frequently referred to as "Southern Ginseng," although it is not closely related to true Panax ginseng. Its adaptogenic constituents include the triterpenoid saponins gypenosides which are closely structurally related to the ginsenosides from the well-known medicinal plant ginseng. It has been shown to lower cholesterol levels in human studies.

Adaptogenic herbs are nontoxic in normal doses, produce a nonspecific defensive response to stress, and have a normalising influence on the body. They normalise the hypothalamic-pituitary-adrenal axis (HPA axis). As defined, adaptogens constitute a new class of natural, homeostatic metabolic regulators. However they are also functional at the level of allostasis which is a more dynamic reaction to long term stress, lacking the fixed reference points of homeostasis. Jiaogulan is a calming adaptogen which is also useful in formula with codonopsis for jet lag and altitude sickness.

Jiaogulan may modulate the nervous system. It calms an overexcited nervous system and stimulates a depressed one. 300 professional athletes were the subjects of a study. All the athletes reported that taking this herb before competition made them vigourous and alert with quick reflexes. Yet it also made them less nervous.

Jiaogulan is also very effective against insomnia - 112 cases of insomnia reported a sleep improvement of 89 to 95 percent – and blood pressure. 223 patients were divided into three groups. One group took Ginseng, the next took Jiaogulan and the last took the blood pressure medication. The effectiveness was rated at 46% for Ginseng, 82% for Jiaogulan and 93% for the synthetic medication. This herb modulates blood pressure, lowering it when it is too high and raising it when it is too low.

Jiaogulan may also increase cardiac function. In a study combined with some other herbs, heart stroke volume increased 37% and cardiac output increased by 21% on the average. Ejection fraction increased by 13%. Subjects had normal blood pressure, which did not change although heart rate decreased by 10%.

Jiaogulan may lower total cholesterol, LDL cholesterol (the "bad" cholesterol), and raises HDL cholesterol (the good one). More than 20 papers have been published on the subject with effectiveness reported as ranging from 67 to 93%. It may also inhibit platelet aggregation, which lessens the chance of a stroke or heart attack and also may increase the production of white blood cells in white cell deficient patients. As an immunostimulant, this herb may modulate lymphocyte formation and increases lymphocyte activity. It was also found to possible enhance the activity of NK (Natural Killer cells). Regarding diabetes, a study of 46 patients with Diabetes Mellitus showed a possible improvement of 89% in their condition. Another study also showed satisfactory results.

As for Hepatitis B, 100 patients were given Jiaogulan for 3 months. Effectiveness was rated at 89%. Another study of 200 patients yielded similar results. Other studies showed the possibility to protect the liver from various toxic chemicals such as carbon tetrachloride. With bronchitis, a study of 86 cases of chronic bronchitis had an effectiveness rate of 93%. Another study of 96 cases had a 92% effectiveness rate.

Jiaogulan works with the circulatory system as it support the body's blood and related systems such as the liver, glands, nerves and general circulation. It supports the immune system, adrenal function, provides energy/metabolism boost, nurtures central nervous system/heart connection, creates unfavourable environment for viruses all of which are also effective against nervous fatigue. Jiaogulan supports the digestive and detoxifying functions of the body, including the urinary system and supports liver health, relieves stress, nourishes the spleen function, supports the pancreas and the cleansing mechanisms of the body by targeting the intestinal, digestive and circulatory systems.

2) **Stinging nettle** (*Urtica dioica*)

Urtica dioica, commonly called stinging nettle, is a herbaceous perennial flowering plant, native to Europe, Asia, northern Africa, and North America, and is the best known member of the nettle genus Urtica. The leaves and stems are very hairy with non-stinging hairs and also bear many stinging hairs (trichomes), whose tips come off when touched, transforming the hair into a needle that will inject several chemicals: acetylcholine, histamine, 5-HT or serotonin, and possibly formic acid. This mixture of chemical compounds cause a sting or paresthesia from which the species derives its common name, as well as the colloquial names burn nettle, burn weed, burn hazel.

A representation of the Stinging Nettle from a herbal compendium

Medicinal uses and scientific research

As Old English Stiðe, nettle is one of the nine plants invoked in the pagan Anglo-Saxon Nine Herbs Charm, recorded in the 10th century. Nettle is believed to be a galactagogue and a clinical trial has shown that the juice is diuretic in patients with congestive heart failure. Urtication, or flogging with nettles, is the process of deliberately applying stinging nettles to the skin in order to provoke inflammation. An agent thus used is known as a rubefacient (i.e. something that causes redness). This is done as a folk remedy for rheumatism, as it provides temporary relief from pain. Extracts can be used to treat arthritis, anaemia, hay fever, kidney problems, and pain.

Cooking, crushing or chopping disables the stinging hairs. Stinging nettle leaves are high in nutrients, and the leaves can be mixed with other ingredients to create a soup rich in calcium and iron. Nettle soup is a good source of nutrients for people who lack meat or fruit in their diets. The young leaves are edible and make a very good pot-herb. The leaves are also dried and may then be used to make a tisane, as can also be done with the nettle's flowers. The high protein content of nettles makes them nutritionally valuable for vegetarians.

Nettle root extracts have been extensively studied in human clinical trials as a treatment for symptoms of benign prostatic hyperplasia (BPH). These extracts have been shown to help relieve symptoms compared to placebo both by themselves and when combined with other herbal medicines. Fresh nettle is used in folk remedies to stop all types of bleeding, due to its high Vitamin K content. Meanwhile, in dry U. dioica, the Vitamin K is practically non-existent, and so is used as a blood thinner.

An extract from the nettle root (Urtica dioica) is used to alleviate symptoms of benign prostate enlargement. Nettle leaf extract, on the other hand, is what has been shown to reduce the pro-inflammatory cytokines TNF-a and IL-B1.

The "above-ground" or aerial parts of nettle may have mild diuretic properties, which means they may promote the loss of water from the body. Recent studies of both humans and laboratory animals confirm that nettle's aerial parts (flowers, leaves, and stems) may increase the production of urine. This diuretic effect may explain why the aerial parts of nettle were formerly used extensively to treat urinary tract conditions such as bladder infections. In Europe, they are still taken along with large quantities of water in a treatment called "irrigation therapy" to force fluids through the urinary system. In fact, they are approved as irrigation therapy for treating urinary tract inflammation and for treating and preventing kidney stones by Commission E of the German Federal Institute for Drugs and Medical Devices, the German governmental agency that evaluates the safety and effectiveness of herbal products. The United States does not have a comparable agency to evaluate herbal products. The aerial parts of nettle are also used to relieve conditions such as premenstrual swelling.

Nettle's aerial parts have been used historically to treat muscle pain and arthritis. Taken orally, products made from nettle's aerial parts may interfere with the body's production of inflammation-causing chemicals--specifically tumour necrosis factor-alpha (TNF-a). Consequently, the aerial parts of nettle may have an anti-inflammatory effect. They may also enhance responses of the immune system. Chemicals in nettle's aerial parts are also thought to reduce the feeling of pain or interfere with the way that nerves send pain signals. All of these effects may reduce the pain and stiffness of arthritis and similar conditions. They may also have some value for relieving other inflammatory conditions such as colitis, which is inflammation of the large intestine.

In addition, nettle's aerial parts may reduce the amount of histamine that is produced by the body in response to an allergen. An allergen is a substance such as pollen that may provoke an exaggerated immune response in individuals who are sensitive to it. Through this potential action, the aerial parts of nettle may help to reduce allergy symptoms.

Very early study results may show that the aerial parts of nettle have positive effects on blood sugar, blood pressure, and blood cholesterol levels. In the past, the aerial parts of nettle plants were thought to raise blood sugar levels slightly. However, in recent studies of laboratory cultures and animals, an extract of nettle leaves has shown the opposite effect. In at least two separate studies that have been reported in recent scientific literature, researchers noted that animals treated with nettle leaf extract produced increased amounts of insulin, thereby reducing blood sugar. In one of the studies, decreased blood sugar occurred in animals with both high and normal blood sugar levels. Some of the animal studies also showed a decrease in blood pressure from nettle's aerial parts, as well - believed at least partially to result from their diuretic effect. Lowered blood pressure was slight and inconsistent, however. Other animal studies have found a cholesterol-reducing effect from nettle leaf extracts.

Either the fresh juice or a solution made from dried aerial parts of nettle may be applied to the skin to relieve joint pain and muscle aches. Astringent properties of nettle aerial parts may also help to relieve the pain of mouth sores, treat acne, lessen the swelling of haemorrhoids, and stop bleeding from minor skin injuries such as razor nicks. An astringent shrinks and tightens the top layers of skin or mucous membranes, thereby reducing secretions, relieving irritation, and improving tissue firmness. Nettle's aerial parts may also be used topically for dandruff and overly oily hair and scalp.

3) Suma (*Pfaffia paniculata*)

Suma is a large, rambling, shrubby ground vine with an intricate, deep, and extensive root system. It is indigenous to the Amazon basin and is traditionally used as a medicine and tonic. Also called nicknamed "para tudo" in Brazil, which means "for all", Suma is an herbal medicine with adaptogenic qualities that serve to normalise and enhance body systems, increase resistance to stress, and boost overall functioning.

Suma's main plant chemicals are: allantoin, beta-ecdysterone, beta-sitosterol, daucosterol, germanium, iron, magnesium, nortriterpenoids, pantothenic acid, pfaffic acids, pfaffosides A-F, polypodine B, saponins, silica, stigmasterol, stigmasterol-3-o-beta-d-glucoside, vitamins A, B1, B2, E, K, and zinc.

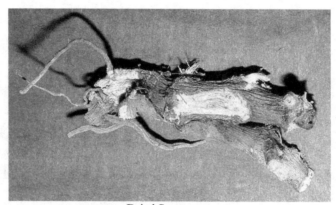
Dried Suma root

Medicinal use and scientific research

The indigenous peoples of the Amazon region have used Suma root for generations for a wide variety of health purposes, including as a general tonic; as an energy, rejuvenating, and sexual tonic; and as a general cure-all for many types of illnesses. Suma has been used as an aphrodisiac, a calming agent, and to treat ulcers for at least 300 years. It is an important herbal remedy in the folk medicine of several rainforest Indian tribes today.

In herbal medicine throughout the world today, Suma is considered a tonic and an adaptogen. The herbal definition of an adaptogen is a plant that increases the body's resistance to adverse influences by a wide range of physical, chemical, and biochemical factors and has a normalising or restorative effect on the body as a whole. In modern Brazilian herbal medicine practices, Suma root is employed as a cellular oxygenator and taken to stimulate appetite and circulation, increase oestrogen production, balance blood sugar levels, enhance the immune system, strengthen the muscular system, and enhance memory.

In North American herbal medicine, Suma root is used as an adaptogenic and regenerative tonic regulating many systems of the body; as an immunostimulant; to treat exhaustion and chronic fatigue, impotence, arthritis, anaemia, diabetes, cancer, tumours, mononucleosis, high blood pressure, PMS, menopause, and hormonal disorders, and many types of stress. In herbal medicine in Ecuador today, Suma is considered a tonic and "normaliser" for the cardiovascular system, the central nervous system, the reproductive system, and the digestive system; it is used to treat hormonal disorders, sexual dysfunction and sterility, arteriosclerosis, diabetes, circulatory and digestive disorders, rheumatism, and bronchitis. Thomas Bartram, in his book Encyclopedia of Herbal Medicine, reports that Suma is used in Europe to restore nerve and glandular functions, to balance the endocrine system, to strengthen the immune system, for infertility, menopausal, and menstrual symptoms, to minimise the side effects of birth control medications, for high cholesterol, to neutralise toxins, and as a general restorative tonic after illness.

Nutritionally, Suma root contains 19 different amino acids, a large number of electrolytes, trace minerals, iron, magnesium, zinc, vitamins A, B1, B2, E, K, and pantothenic acid. Its high germanium content probably accounts for its properties as an oxygenator at the cellular level; its high iron content may account for its traditional use for anaemia. The root also contains novel phytochemicals including saponins, pfaffic acids, glycosides, and nortriterpenes.

Suma has also been called "the Russian secret," as it has been taken by Russian Olympic athletes for many years and has been reported to increase muscle-building and endurance without the side effects associated with steroids. This action is attributed to an anabolic-type phytochemical called beta-ecdysterone and three novel ecdysteroid glycosides that are found in high amounts in Suma. Suma is such a rich source of beta-ecdysterone that it is the subject of a Japanese patent for the extraction methods employed to obtain it from Suma root (approximately 2.5 g of bcta-ecdysterone can be extracted from 400 g of powdered Suma root-or .63%). These same Japanese researchers filed a U.S. patent in 1998 for a proprietary extract of Suma (which extracted the ecdysterone and beta-ecdysterone); it claimed (through various in vivo and in vitro studies) that their compound maintained health, enhanced the immune system, and had a tonic and an anti-allergenic effect. A French company also filed a U.S. patent on the topical use of these ecdysterone chemicals, claiming that their Suma ecdysterone extract strengthened the water barrier function of the skin, increased skin keratinocyte differentiation (which would be helpful for psoriasis), gave the skin a smoother, softer appearance and, also, improved hair appearance.

Suma root has a very high saponin content (up to 11%). In phytochemistry, plant saponins are well known to have a wide spectrum of activities including lowering blood cholesterol, inhibiting cancer cell growth, and acting as antifungal and antibacterial agents. They are also known as natural detergent and foaming agents. Phytochemists report that saponins can act by binding with bile acids and cholesterol. It is thought that these chemicals "clean" or purge these fatty compounds from the body (thus lowering blood cholesterol levels).

The specific saponins found in the roots of Suma include a group of novel phytochemicals that scientists have named pfaffosides. These saponins have clinically demonstrated the ability to inhibit cultured tumour cell melanomas (in vitro) and help to regulate blood sugar levels (in vivo). The pfaffosides and pfaffic acid derivatives in Suma were patented as antitumour compounds in several Japanese patents in the mid-1980s. In a study described in one of the patents, researchers reported that an oral dosage of 100 mg/kg (of Suma saponins) given to rats was active against abdominal cancer. The other patents and Japanese research report that the pfaffic acids found in Suma root had a strong in vitro activity against melanoma, liver carcinoma, and lung carcinoma cells at only 4-6 mcg of pfaffic acids.

In addition to the pfaffic acids having anticancerous activity, research in Japan (in 2000) reported that natural Suma root had anti-cancerous activity as well. In this in vivo study, an oral administration of powdered Suma root (at a dosages of 750 mg/kg) was reported to inhibit the proliferation of lymphoma and leukaemia in mice and, otherwise, delay mortality. Notice, however, that this antiproliferative effect slowed the growth of these cancer cells - it did not eradicate them. These researchers postulated that the inhibitory effect evidenced might be due to the enhancement of the nonspecific and/or cellular immune systems.

In 1995, another U.S. patent was filed which detailed some beneficial effects of Suma root against sickle-cell anaemia. In a double blind placebo human study, they reported that 15 patients taking Suma root for three months (1000 mg three times daily) increased hemoglobin levels, inhibited red blood cell sickling and, generally, improved their physical condition by reducing side effects during the treatment. These results were statistically higher than the 15 other patients on placebo. Unfortunately, once treatment was discontinued, symptoms and blood parameters returned to their pretreated state within 3-6 months. It was reported, however, that several patients in the study remained on the Suma supplement for three years or longer. They reportedly maintained consistent improvement and a higher quality of life with no side effects. Other U.S. researchers (in 2000) studied Suma root's actual mechanism of action in its ability to resickle blood cells and reported their findings-which again confirmed an antisickling effect and a rehydration effect of sickled cells (in vitro).

In other research, Suma demonstrated analgesic and anti-inflammatory activities in various in vivo rat and mouse studies. Another tested activity focused on its long history of use as a sexual stimulant and aphrodisiac. Researchers verified this traditional use, reporting in a 1999 clinical study that a Suma root extract was able to increase the sexual performance in healthy, sexually sluggish and impotent rats. In 2001, a U.S. patent was filed on a multi-plant combination containing Suma for sexual enhancement in humans. The patent indicated that the Suma extract tested increased sexual performance and function.

4) **Pau d'Arco** (*genus Tabebuia*)

The Tabebuia genus is native from South America and the wood is used for furniture, decking, and other outdoor uses. It is increasingly popular as a decking material due to its insect resistance and durability. Tabebuia is widely used as ornamental tree in the tropics in landscaping gardens, public squares and boulevards due to its impressive and colourful flowering. Many flowers appear on still leafless stems at the end of the dry season, making the floral display more conspicuous. They are useful as honey plants for bees, and are popular with certain hummingbirds.

Pau d'Arco flowers

Medicinal use and scientific research

The bark of several species has medical properties. The bark is dried, shredded and then boiled making a bitter or sour-tasting brownish-coloured tea. Tea from the inner bark of Pink Ipê (T. impetiginosa) is known as Lapacho or Taheebo. Its main active principles are lapachol, quercetin and other flavonoids. It is also available in pill form. The herbal remedy is typically used during flu and cold season and for easing smoker's cough. It apparently works as expectorant, by promoting the lungs to cough up and free deeply embedded mucus and contaminants. Tabebuia heteropoda, T. incana and other species are occasionally used as an additive to the entheogenic drink Ayahuasca.

In the laboratory, chemicals derived from Pau d'Arco have been studied for treating a number of conditions. One chemical known as lapachol has been shown active against the parasite that causes malaria. Lapachol also seems to inhibit Herpes simplex, the virus that causes cold sores. At low doses, chemicals in Pau d'Arco may help to activate the immune system and lapachol and other chemicals in Pau d'Arco may be active against other parasites and viruses.

Topically, Pau d'Arco appears to have varying amounts of antibacterial, antifungal, antiprotozoal, and antiviral properties. In Central American and South American countries, Pau d'Arco is used topically to treat minor skin injuries, such as insect bites, as well as more serious conditions such as psoriasis. It has also been used as a mouthwash and to treat vaginal yeast infections.

Pau d'Arco has a long and well-documented history of use by the indigenous peoples of the rainforest. Indications imply that its use may actually predate the Incas. Throughout South America, tribes living thousands of miles apart have employed it for the same medicinal purposes for hundreds of years. Several Indian tribes of the rainforest have used Pau d'Arco wood for centuries to make their hunting bows; their common names for the tree mean "bow stick" and "bow stem." The Guarani and Tupi Indians call the tree tajy, which means "to have strength and vigour." They use the bark to treat many different conditions and as a tonic for the same strength and vigour it puts into their bows. Pau d'Arco is recorded to be used by forest inhabitants throughout the Amazon for malaria, anaemia, colitis, respiratory problems, colds, cough, flu, fungal infections, fever, arthritis and rheumatism, snakebite, poor circulation, boils, syphilis, and cancer amongst many others.

The chemical constituents and active ingredients of Pau d'Arco have been well documented. Its use with (and reported cures for) various types of cancers fueled much of the early research in the early 1960s. The plant contains a large amount of chemicals known as quinoids, and a small quantity of benzenoids and flavonoids. These quinoids (and, chiefly, anthraquinones, furanonaphthoquinones, lapachones, and naphthoquinones) have shown the most documented biological activity and are seen to be the centre of the plant's efficacy as an herbal remedy. In the 1960s, plant extracts of the heartwood and bark demonstrated marked antitumourous effects in animals, which drew the interest of the National Cancer Institute (NCI). Researchers decided that the most potent single chemical for this activity was a naphthoquinone chemical named lapachol and they concentrated solely on this single chemical in their subsequent cancer research. In a 1968 study, lapachol demonstrated highly significant activity against cancerous tumours in rats.

By 1970, NCI-backed research already was testing lapachol in human cancer patients. The institute reported, however, that their first Phase I study failed to produce a therapeutic effect without side-effects - and they discontinued further cancer research shortly thereafter. These side-effects were nausea and vomiting (very common with chemotherapy drugs) and anti-vitamin K activity (the main concerns over which caused anaemia and an anticoagulation effect). Interestingly, other chemicals in the whole plant extract (which, initially, showed positive antitumour effects and very low toxicity) demonstrated positive effects on vitamin

K and, conceivably, compensated for lapachol's negative effect. Instead of pursuing research on a complex combination of at least 20 active chemicals in a whole plant extract (several of which had antitumour effects and other positive biological activities), research focused on a single, patentable chemical-and it didn't work as well. Despite NCI's abandonment of the research, another group developed a lapachol analog (which was patentable) in 1975. One study reported that this lapachol analog increased the life span of mice inoculated with leukaemic cells by over 80%. In a small, uncontrolled, 1980 study of nine human patients with various cancers (liver, kidney, breast, prostate, and cervix), pure lapachol was reported to shrink tumours and reduce pain caused by them - and three of the patients realised complete remissions.

The phytochemical database housed at the U.S. Department of Agriculture has documented lapachol as being antiabscess, anticarcinomic, antiedemic, anti-inflammatory, antimalarial, antiseptic, antitumourous, antiviral, bactericidal, fungicidal, insectifugal, pesticidal, protisticidal, respiratory depressant, schistosomicidal, termiticidal, and viricidal. It's not surprising that Pau d'Arco's beneficial effects were seen to stem from its lapachol content. But another chemical in Pau d'Arco, beta-lapachone, has been studied closely of late-and a number of recent patents have been filed on it. It has demonstrated in laboratory studies to have activities similar to lapachol (antimicrobial, antifungal, antiviral, antitumourous, antileukaemic, and anti-inflammatory), with few side-effects. In one of these studies on beta-lapachone and other quinones in Pau d'Arco, researchers reported: "Because of their potent activity against the growth of human keratinocytes, some lapachol-derived compounds appear to be promising as effective antipsoriatic agents. In a 2002 U.S. patent, beta-lapachone was cited to have significant anticancerous activity against human cancer cell lines including: promyelocytic leukaemia, prostate, malignant glioma, colon, hepatoma, breast, ovarian, pancreatic, multiple myeloma cell lines and drug-resistant cell lines. In yet another U.S. patent, beta-lapachone was cited with the in vivo ability to inhibit the growth of prostate tumours.

In addition to its reported antitumour and antileukaemic activities, Pau d'Arco clearly has demonstrated broad spectrum actions against a number of disease-causing microorganisms, which supports its wide array of uses in herbal medicine. Antimicrobial properties of many of Pau d'Arco's active phytochemicals were demonstrated in several clinical studies, in which they exhibited strong in vitro activity against bacteria, fungi, and yeast (including Candida, Aspergillus, Staphylococcus, Streptococcus, Helicobacter pylori, Brucella, tuberculosis, pneumonia, and dysentery). In addition to its isolated chemicals, a hot water extract of Pau d'Arco demonstrated antibacterial actions against Staphylococcus aureus, Helicobacter pylori (the bacteria that commonly causes stomach ulcers), and Brucella. A water extract of Pau d'Arco was reported (in other in vitro clinical research) to have strong activity against 11 fungus and yeast strains. Pau d'Arco and its chemicals also have demonstrated in vitro antiviral properties against various viruses, including Herpes I and II, influenza, polio virus, and vesicular stomatitis virus. Its antiparasitic actions against various parasites (including malaria, schistosoma, and trypanosoma) have been confirmed as well. Finally, bark extracts of Pau d'Arco have demonstrated anti-inflammatory activity and have shown success against a wide range of induced inflammation in mice and rats.

5) **Elderflower** (*Sambucus nigra*)

The flowers of Sambucus nigra are used to produce elderflower liqueur. Ornamental varieties of Sambucus are grown in gardens and hollowed elderberry twigs have traditionally been used as spiles to tap maple trees for syrup.

The Elder Tree was supposed to ward off evil influence and give protection from witches, a popular belief held in widely-distant countries. If an elder tree was cut down, a spirit known as the Elder Mother would be released and teach the culprit a lesson. The tree could only safely be cut while chanting a rhyme to the Elder Mother.

Medicinal uses and scientific research

European elder grows up to 30 feet tall, is native to Europe, but has been naturalised to the Americas. Historically, the flowers and leaves have been used for pain relief, swelling/inflammation, diuresis (urine production), and as a diaphoretic or expectorant. The leaves have been used externally for sitz baths. The bark, when aged, has been used as a diuretic, laxative, or emetic (to induce vomiting). The berries have been used traditionally in food as flavouring and in the preparation of elderberry wine and pies. Native Americans used the flowers, berries, and bark of elderberry trees to treat fevers and joint pain for hundreds of years, but elderberry's real claim to fame is as a cure for the flu.

The flowers and berries (blue/black only) are used most often medicinally. They contain flavonoids, which are found to possess a variety of actions, including antioxidant and immunologic properties. Elderflowers constituents are, potassium nitrate, sambucin, sambunigrin and sugars. The complex sugars of the leaf are the immune-active fraction. Extensive research show that elder stop the production of hormone-like cytokines that direct a class of white blood cells known as neutrophils to cause inflammation, especially in influenza and arthritis.

Elder berries are known to be effective against eight strains of influenza. This suggests that elder be superior to vaccines in preventing flu, because flu vaccines are only effective against known strains of flu, whereas the virus is continually mutating to new strains. Vaccines have another draw back: over half of people who get them report side effects.

Dr. Madeleine Mumcuoglu, of Hadassah-Hebrew University in Israel found that elderberry disarms the enzyme viruses use to penetrate healthy cells in the lining of the nose and throat. Taken before infection, it prevents infection. Taken after infection, it prevents spread of the virus through the respiratory tract.

Elder Flowers

In a clinical trial, 20% of study subjects reported significant improvement within 24 hours, 70% by 48 hours, and 90% claimed complete cure in three days. In contrast, subjects receiving the placebo required 6 days to recover.

Elder has been observed to reduce excessive sinus mucus secretion in laboratory studies. There is only limited research specifically using elder to treat sinusitis in humans. Combination products containing elder and other herbs have been reported to have beneficial effects when used with antibiotics to treat sinus infections. Early study reports that elderberry juice may decrease serum cholesterol concentrations and increase low-density lipoprotein (LDL or "bad" cholesterol) stability.

6) **Sea-Buckthorn** (*Hippophae L.*)

There are 6 species and 12 subspecies of Sea-Buckthorn native over a wide area of Europe and Asia. More than 90 percent or about 1.5 million hectares of the world's sea buckthorn resources can be found in China where the plant is exploited for soil and water conservation purposes. They are tolerant of salt in the air and soil, but demand full sunlight for good growth and do not tolerate shady conditions near larger trees. The common Sea-Buckthorn (Hippophae rhamnoides) is by far the most widespread, with a range extending from the Atlantic coasts of Europe right across to northwestern China.

Sea Buckthorn leaves and fruit

Medicinal uses and scientific research

Nutrient and phytochemical constituents of Sea-Buckthorn berries have potential value as antioxidants that may affect inflammatory disorders, cancer or other diseases, although no specific health benefits have yet been proved by clinical research in humans.

The fruit of the plant has a high vitamin C content—in a range of 114 to 1550 mg per 100 grams with an average content (695 mg per 100 grams) about 12 times greater than the 50 mg of vitamin C per 100 grams found in orange— placing Sea-Buckthorn fruit among the most enriched plant sources of vitamin C. The fruit also contains dense contents of carotenoids, vitamin E, amino acids, dietary minerals, beta-sitosterol and polyphenolic acids.

Different parts of Sea-Buckthorn have been used as traditional therapies for diseases but such knowledge remains mostly unreferenced outside of Asia and is communicated mainly from person to person.

Grown widely throughout its native China and other mainland regions of Asia, Sea-Buckthorn is an herbal medicine used over centuries to relieve cough, aid digestion, invigorate blood circulation and alleviate pain. In Mongolia, extracts of Sea-Buckthorn branches and leaves are used to treat gastrointestinal distress in humans and animals. Bark and leaves are used for treating diarrhoea, gastrointestinal, dermatologic disorders and topical compressions for rheumatoid arthritis. Flowers may be used as a skin softener.

For its hemostatic and anti-inflammatory effects, berry fruits are added to medications for pulmonary, gastrointestinal, cardiac, blood and metabolic disorders in Indian, Chinese and Tibetan medicines. Sea-Buckthorn berry components have potential anticarcinogenic activity and other studies - including recent releases in some of the scientific journals in Europe, the US and Russia - have shown Sea Buckthorn helps battle the harmful effects of radiation thanks to its antioxidant properties, which protect against inflammation and free radicals, especially those produced by radiation. This is why it was given to cosmonauts in early Russian missions into space.

Fresh juice, syrup and berry or seed oils are used for colds, fever, exhaustion, as an analgesic or treatment for stomach ulcers, cancer, and metabolic disorders. Called 'Chharma' in some native languages, oil from fruits and seeds is used for liver diseases, inflammation, disorders of the gastrointestinal system, including peptic ulcers and gastritis, eczema, canker sores and other ulcerative disorders of mucosal tissues, wounds, inflammation, burns, frostbite, psoriasis, rosacea, lupus erythematosus, and chronic dermatoses. In ophthalmology, berry extracts have been used for keratosis, trachoma, eyelid injuries and conjunctivitis. As an internal dietary supplement It has shown to help promote healthy blood circulation, the rudimentary treatment of colitis, stomach ulcers, and as soothing agent for the gastro-intestinal tract.

Sara Stanner, a nutritionist at the British Heart Foundation has been quoted to say, "The antioxidants in sea buckthorn juice and pulp may protect the heart by reducing harmful chemicals in the blood. The pulp oil also contains unsaturated fatty acids and plant sterols, which could help to reduce blood cholesterol levels. In addition, there is evidence that sea buckthorn juice might help to protect 'bad' cholesterol from oxidation, a process that is involved in the development of coronary heart disease. The oil has also been shown to have a possible benefit in reducing the tendency of blood to clot but more research is needed to clarify whether adding it to foods can have any real impact on reducing risk of heart disease."

7) Cat's Claw (*Uncaria tomentosa*)

Uncaria tomentosa (popularly known in English as Cat's Claw, in Spanish as Uña de Gato or as Indian name Vilcacora) is a woody vine found in the tropical jungles of South and Central America, which derives its name from hook-like thorns that resemble the claws of a cat. U. tomentosa can grow up to 30m tall, climbing by means of these thorns. It is used as an alternative medicine in the treatment of a variety of ailments.

Cat's Claw leaves and characteristic "claws".

Medicinal use and scientific research

The parts used medicinally include the inner bark and root, taken in the form of capsules, tea and extract. Cat's Claw is used in nootropic drugs, as well as in treatment of cancer and HIV infection. It contains several alkaloids that are responsible for its overall medical effects, as well as tannins and various phytochemicals. Some ingredients appear to act as anti-inflammatory, antioxidant and anticancer agents.

Dr. Brent Davis, D.C. has written several articles on cat's claw and refers to it as the "opener of the way" for its ability to cleanse the entire intestinal tract and its effectiveness in treating intestinal ailments such as Crohn's disease, gastric ulcers and tumours, parasites, colitis, gastritis, diverticulitis and leaky bowel syndrome, while manufacturers claim that U. tomentosa can also be used in the treatment of

AIDS in combination with AZT, the treatment and prevention of arthritis and rheumatism, diabetes, PMS, chronic fatigue syndrome, prostate conditions, immune modulation, Lyme disease and systemic lupus erythematosus. A 2005 review of the scholarly literature on Cat's Claw, including reports from Dr. Julian Whitaker, M.D. indicates there is supporting evidence toward its use in treating cancer, inflammation, viral infection and vascular conditions, and for its use as an immunostimulant, antioxidant, antibacterial and CNS-related agent.

Both South American Uncaria species are used by the indigenous peoples of the Amazon rainforest in very similar ways and have long histories of use. Cat's claw (U. tomentosa) has been used medicinally by the Aguaruna, Asháninka, Cashibo, Conibo, and Shipibo tribes of Peru for at least 2,000 years. The Asháninka Indian tribe in central Peru has the longest recorded history of use of the plant. They are also the largest commercial source of cat's claw from Peru today. The Asháninka use cat's claw to treat asthma, inflammations of the urinary tract, arthritis, rheumatism, and bone pain, to recover from childbirth, as a kidney cleanser, to cure deep wounds, to control inflammation and gastric ulcers and for cancer. Indigenous tribes in Piura use cat's claw to treat tumours, inflammations, rheumatism, and gastric ulcers.

Other Peruvian indigenous tribes use cat's claw to treat diabetes, urinary tract cancer in women, haemorrhages, menstrual irregularity, cirrhosis, fevers, abscesses, gastritis, rheumatism, tumours, and inflammations as well as for internal cleansing and to "normalise the body." Reportedly, cat's claw has also been used as a contraceptive by several different tribes of Peru (but only in very large dosages). Dr. Fernando Cabieses, M.D., a noted authority on Peruvian medicinal plants, explains that the Asháninka boil 5 to 6 kg (about 12 pounds) of the root in water until it is reduced to little more than 1 cup. This decoction is then taken 1 cup daily during the period of menstruation for three consecutive months; this supposedly causes sterility for three to four years.

Cat's claw has been used in Peru and Europe since the early 1990s as an adjunctive treatment for cancer and AIDS as well as for other diseases that target the immune system. In herbal medicine today, cat's claw is employed around the world for many different conditions, including immune disorders, gastritis, ulcers, cancer, arthritis, rheumatism, rheumatic disorders, neuralgias, chronic inflammation of all kinds, and such viral diseases as herpes zoster (shingles).

Probably the best-researched use of cat's claw is for the relief of pain associated with both osteoarthritis (OA) and rheumatoid arthritis (RA). Results from animal studies and reports of human cases show that taking cat's claw by mouth may have anti-inflammatory effects for individuals with OA (the deterioration of joints due to wear and tear) or RA (an autoimmune disease in which the body's immune system attacks cartilage and synovial fluid in joints). Although the reasons are not all known, chemicals in cat's claw are believed to block the production of substances such as prostaglandins and tumour necrosis factor (TNF) alpha, which are involved in inflammation.

Various chemicals that it contains are known to promote the loss of water from the body, relax smooth muscles, and widen small blood vessels in the hands and feet. All these effects may help to lower blood pressure. Cat's claw may have immune-system effects, as well. One theory is that chemicals in it promote the activity of macrophages, which are specialised white blood cells that absorb bacteria and tumour cells and also activate other immune system cells. In animal studies, cat's claw also appeared to promote the production of chemicals that extended the active lives of lymphocytes (white blood cells that fight infection). Lymphocyte production was not increased, however. In other laboratory studies, cat's claw extract stopped the spread of human lymphoma, leukaemia, and breast cancer cells. In one small human study and several animal studies, taking cat's claw may have promoted the repair of DNA damaged by chemotherapy or radiation.

8) **Maitake** (*Grifola frondosa*)

Grifola frondosa, referring to a mythical griffin, commonly known as Sheep's Head, Ram's Head and Hen of the Woods or Maitake, is an edible polypore mushroom. It grows in clusters at the foot of trees, especially oak. The fungus is native to the northeastern part of Japan and North America, and is prized in traditional Chinese and Japanese herbology as an adaptogen, an aid to balance out altered body systems to a normal level. Most Japanese people find its taste and texture enormously appealing.

Maitake, an edible mushroom of the (Polyporaceae) family, can grow up to over 50 pounds (20 kilograms), earning this giant mushroom the title "King of Mushroom". In Japan, Maitake make up the 4 or so major mushrooms used in the country (the others being shiitake, shimeji and enoki). They are used in a wide variety of dishes, often being a key ingredient in nabe or cooked in foil with butter.

The Japanese word "Maitake" means dancing mushroom because people in ancient times were said to dance for joy when they found these mushrooms - the mushrooms were literally worth their weight in silver. Modern research on the Maitake mushroom and its D-fraction extract began in Japan in the mid-1980s and has only recently spread to the United States.

As of the early 21st century, much has been written about Maitake and its magic healing qualities. This has sparked a great deal of interest in its use for various human illnesses.

Medicinal use and scientific research

The underground tubers from which Maitake arises has been used in traditional Chinese and Japanese medicine to enhance the immune system. Researchers have also indicated that whole Maitake has the ability to regulate blood pressure, glucose, insulin, and both serum and liver lipids, such as cholesterol, triglycerides, and phospholipids, and may also be useful for weight loss.

Maitake is rich in minerals (such as potassium, calcium, and magnesium), various vitamins (B2, D2 and Niacin), fibres and amino acids. It also provides nutritional support by enhancing the colon's ability to absorb micronutrients, especially copper and zinc. The active constituent in Maitake for enhancing the immune activity has been identified in the late 1980s to be the protein-bound polysaccharide compound, beta-glucan, an ingredient found especially in the family of polyporaceae.

According to the American Cancer Society, Maitake has proven itself to be an effective cancer fighter. In laboratory tests, powdered Maitake increased the activity of three types of immune cells-macrophages, natural killer (NIK) cells, and T cells by 140, 186, and 160 percent, respectively. A Chinese clinical study established that Maitake treatment reduces the recurrence of bladder surgery from 65 to 33 percent. Researchers have found that Maitake, when combined with the standard chemotherapy drug mitomycin (Mutamycin), inhibits the growth of breast caner cells, even after metastasis.

Maitake mushroom

Maitake also protects the liver. Chinese doctors conducted a controlled trial with thirty-two patients who had chronic hepatitis B. The recovery rate was 72 percent in the Maitake treatment group, compared with 57 percent in the control group. Hepatitis antigens disappeared in more than 40 percent of the Maitake patients, indicating the virus had been purged from the liver.

Laboratory studies also show that Maitake protects liver tissue from hepatitis caused by environmental toxins such as carbon tetrachloride and paracematol. These compounds go through a two-step process in the liver in which they are first activated into toxic forms and then deactivated into harmless forms. Since Maitake helps the liver handle chemical poisons in both steps, it protects this organ against a broad range of potential toxins.

D-fraction (the extract from Maitake) contains a polysaccharide called beta-glucan (sometimes called beta-glycan) that is found in several mushrooms, yeasts, and other foods. A polysaccharide is a large and complex molecule made up of smaller sugar molecules (similar to the lentinan in shiitake mushrooms; see Shiitake Mushroom). The beta-glucan polysaccharide is believed to stimulate the immune system and activate certain cells and proteins that attack cancer, including macrophages, T-cells, and natural killer cells (types of white blood cells) and interleukin-1 and -2. In lab studies, it appears to slow the growth of cancer in some cell cultures and in mice.

Most of the research on Maitake D-fraction has been done in Japan using an injectable form of the extract. A 1997 study published in the Annals of the New York Academy of Science found that Maitake D-fraction extract was able to enhance the immune system and inhibit the spread of tumours in mice that had been implanted with breast cancer. In a 1995 report published in the same journal, researchers concluded that Maitake D-fraction extract was able to activate the immune response in mice injected with liver cancer cells to prevent the spread of tumours to the liver, and prevent the development of cancer in normal cells.

In another clinical trial, beta-glucan is being tested along with other drugs to learn if they increase the effectiveness of another monoclonal antibody (3F8). Combining different types of biological therapy may kill more tumour cells. This is a small open label trial in patients with neuroblastoma that has not responded to treatment. A trial of Maitake extract as treatment for breast cancer is also in progress.

The results of a study by the Kobe Pharmaceutical University in Japan suggest that MD-Fraction obtained from Maitake inhibits tumour metastasis by activating NK cells and APCs, and by suppressing of ICAM-1 leading to the inhibition of tumour cell adhesion to vascular endothelial cells. Another study from the same University concluded that Maitake MD-fraction containing beta-1,6 glucan with beta-1,3 branched chains had previously exhibited strong anticancer activity by increasing immune-competent cell activity. In this non-random case series, a combination of MD-fraction and whole Maitake powder was investigated to determine its effectiveness for 22- to 57-year-old cancer patients in stages II-IV. Cancer regression or significant symptom improvement was observed in 58.3 percent of liver cancer patients, 68.8 percent of breast cancer patients, and 62.5 percent of lung cancer patients. The trial found a less than 10-20 percent improvement for leukaemia, stomach cancer, and brain cancer patients. Furthermore, when Maitake was taken in addition to chemotherapy, immune-competent cell activities were enhanced 1.2-1.4 times, compared with chemotherapy alone. Animal studies have supported the use of Maitake MD-fraction for cancer.

9) **Reishi** (*Ganoderma lucidum*)

Reishi (in Japanese) and Linghzhi (in Chinese) are the names for one form of the mushroom Ganoderma lucidum, and its close relative Ganoderma tsugae, which grows in the northern Eastern Hemlock forests. Ganoderma lucidum enjoys special veneration in Asia, where it has been used in traditional Chinese medicine as a herbal medicine for more than 4,000 years, making it one of the oldest mushrooms known to have been used in medicine. Similar species of Ganoderma have been found growing in the Amazon, according to Christopher Hobbs.

The word Lingzhi, in Chinese, means "herb of spiritual potency" and has also been described as "mushroom of immortality". Because of its presumed health benefits and apparent absence of side-effects, it has attained a reputation in the East as the ultimate herbal substance. Reishi has now been added to the American Herbal Pharmacopoeia and Therapeutic Compendium.

The name Ganoderma is derived from the Greek ganos "brightness, sheen", hence "shining" and derma "skin", while the specific epithet lucidum in Latin for "shining" and tsugae refers to being of the Hemlock (Tsuga). Another Japanese name is mannentake, meaning "10 000 year mushroom". In nature, Reishi grows at the base and stumps of deciduous trees, especially maple. Only two or three out of 10,000 such aged trees will have Reishi growth, and therefore its wild form is generally rare. Today, Reishi is effectively cultivated both indoors under sterile conditions and outdoors on either logs or woodchip beds.

There are multiple species of Reishi, scientifically known to be within the Ganoderma lucidum species complex and mycologists are still researching the differences between species within this complex of species. Ganoderma lucidum is the only known source of a group of triterpenes, known as ganoderic acids, which have a molecular structure similar to steroid hormones. It is a source of biologically active polysaccharides with presumed medicinal properties, and it also contains, ergosterol, coumarin, mannitol, lactones, alkaloids, unsaturated fatty acids, vitamins and minerals. Unlike many other mushrooms, which have up to 90% water content, fresh Reishi only contains about 75% water.

Medicinal use and scientific research

The Shen Nong's Herbal Classic, a 2000-year old medicinal Chinese book considered today as the oldest book on oriental herbal medicine, classifies 365 species of roots, grass, woods, furs, animals and stones into three categories of herbal medicine. Reishi ranked number one of the first category - superior medicines - and was therefore the most exalted medicine in ancient times.

The anti-tumoural effect of Reishi is not entirely known but it is probably due to a combination of different mechanisms: inhibition of the angiogenesis (formation of arterial vessels that give nutrients to the tumour) by mediating over the cytoquines, inducing and enhancing the apoptosis of tumoural cells (the natural and spontaneous cellular death). There are probably other mechanisms involved in the antitumoural action of Reishi such as its inhibitory effect over the growth of cells containing masculine or feminine hormonal receptors (androgens and oestrogens), being this of particular interest when dealing with breast cancer or prostate cancer.

Reishi mushrooms

Other possible mechanism of action that could explain the antitumoural effect of Reishi such as a direct citotoxic effect on the tumoural cells has also been postulated. It has also been suggested that Reishi could act blocking and stopping the migration of the cancer cells and therefore delaying the presence of metastasis. It seems that all these mechanisms could explain, at least in part, the positive effect of Ganoderma Lucidum in breast -, prostate-, lung-, colon- and rectum cancer as well as in other forms.

It is understood as adaptogenic, anti-allergenic and anti-hypertensive due to the presence of triterpenes. Apart from these properties, Reishi has been found to be anti-inflammatory, antiviral, anti-parasitic, anti-fungal, antidiabetic, anti-hypotensive, and protective of the liver. It has also been found to inhibit platelet aggregation, and to lower blood pressure, cholesterol and blood sugar.

Because of these properties, Reishi has been regarded as blood pressure stabiliser, antioxidant, analgesic, a kidney and nerve tonic. It has been used in bronchitis prevention and in cardiovascular treatment, and in the treatment of high triglycerides, high blood pressure, hepatitis, allergies, chemotherapy support, HIV support, and even for fatigue and altitude sickness. Some peer-reviewed studies indicate that ganoderic acid has some protective effects against liver injury by viruses and other toxic agents in mice, suggesting a potential benefit of this compound in the treatment of liver diseases in humans.

Although the experiences in fighting cancer are more inconsistent, the extract has been claimed to be effective in regressing tumours. The results depend on the type of cancer and the severity of the condition. It is usually recommended that it be used in combination with other prescribed medical treatments and as part of a fu zheng formula with a variety of supporting herbs. The Ganoderma extract has been employed to help substantially reduce or eliminate the side-effects of radio- and chemotherapies if it is taken before, during and after the treatments. It has been found clinically to reduce side-effects like hair loss, nausea, vomiting, stomatitis, sore throat, loss of appetite and insomnia.

Observations have shown that Reishi generally has only slight side effects and can be consumed in high doses, in parallel with other medications. Its main properties are adaptogenic, which mean that it is nontoxic, it works in a generalised manner on the hypothalamic-pituitary-adrenal axis and the neuroendocrine system. Its actions are alterative, enhance the immune system and lessen nervous tension. These properties are conducive to normalising and balancing the body (homeostasis and allostasis), and as a result, Reishi is able to help the body cure a multitude of disease states from within.

Reishi has been found to strengthen the respiratory system and to have a healing effect on the lungs, and is particularly beneficial for individuals with asthma, cough and other respiratory complaints. At least one population study conducted in the 1970s confirms this claim. When more than 2,000 Chinese with chronic bronchitis took Reishi syrup, 60 to 90% felt better within two weeks and reported an improved appetite, according to an article entitled, Medicinal Mushrooms, written by Christopher Hobbs, and published in Herbs for Health, Jan/February 97.

In Japan, after daily injections in mice with cancer it was reported that tumours in 50% of the animals had completely regressed within 10 days (Ikekawa et al,1968;Japanese Journal of Cancer Research; 59: 155-157). The host-dependent anti-tumour activity has been subsequently confirmed to be from the polysaccharide fractions of Ganoderma by Sasaki et al. Multiple similar studies subsequently confirm this observation and anti-tumour efficacy of Ganoderma has been demonstrated from various species, at different stages of growth and using different solvents for extraction and different routes of administration. Anti-tumour activity has been demonstrated in vitro as well as in syngeneic tumour systems in animals. However, no human trials of Ganoderma against cancer in peer reviewed journals nor any controlled clinical trials in humans have yet been conducted or published.

A recent study by the Graduate Institute of Medical Sciences from Taipei Medical University in Taiwan investigated the inhibitory activity and explored the molecular mechanisms of anti-tumour effect on colorectal cancer cells in vitro and in vivo as well as tested the side effects of Reishi. The results were that Reishi extracts inhibit colorectal cancer cell proliferation caused by accumulating cells in G(2)/M phase, and it may be through downregulation of cyclin A and B1 and upregulation of p21 and p27. tumourigenesis study in nude mice revealed the extracts caused tumour shrinkage. Additionally, safety assay showed Reishi extracts caused no significant side effects in an animal model. As a conclusion, this study provides molecular evidence that Reishi extracts exert anti-tumour effects both in vitro and in vivo on colorectal adenocarcinoma cells by inducing G(2)/M cell cycle arrest. More importantly, no significant physiological changes resulting from treatment with Reishi extracts were observed in the animal model. Therefore, these data provide new insights into the possible therapeutic use of Reishi for treating colorectal cancer.

Another recent study from the Sinai Medical Center from the David Geffen School of Medicine at UCLA in the United States of America published in 2006, screened a Reishi extract for its anti-proliferative activity using a panel of 36 human cancer cell lines. After exposure to the Reishi extract, HL-60 cells became multinucleated with an increased DNA content. These results indicate that the Reishi extract has a profound activity against leukaemia, lymphoma and multiple myeloma cells and may be a novel adjunctive therapy for the treatment of hematologic malignancies.

10) **Shiitake** (*Lentinula edodes*)

The Shiitake is an edible mushroom native to East Asia, which is cultivated and consumed in many Asian countries, as well as being dried and exported to many countries around the world. It is a feature of many Asian cuisines including Chinese, Japanese, Korean and Thai. In the East, the Shiitake mushroom has long been considered a delicacy as well as a medicinal mushroom.

It is generally known in the English-speaking world by its Japanese name, shiitake, literally "shii mushroom", from the Japanese name of the tree that provides the dead logs on which it is typically cultivated.

In Chinese, it is called xianggu, literally "fragrant mushroom". Two Chinese variant names for high grades of shiitake are donggu, "winter mushroom" and huagu, "flower mushroom", which has a flower-like cracking pattern on the mushroom's upper surface. Both are produced at colder temperatures. Other names by which the mushroom is known in English include Chinese black mushroom and black forest mushroom. In Korean it is called pyogo, in Thai they are called hed hom, "fragrant mushroom", and in Vietnamese they are called nam huong, also "fragrant mushroom".

The species was formerly known as Lentinus edodes and Agaricus edodes. The latter name was first applied by the English botanist Miles Joseph Berkeley in 1878.

Shiitake growing on a log

History

Shiitake are native to China but have been grown in both Japan and China since prehistoric times. They have been cultivated for over 1,000 years; the first written record of shiitake cultivation can be traced to Wu Sang Guang, born during the

Song Dynasty (AD 960–1127). However, some documents record the uncultivated mushroom being eaten as early as AD 199.

During the Ming Dynasty (AD 1368–1644), physician Wu Juei wrote that the mushroom could be used not only as a food but as a medicinal mushroom, taken as a remedy for upper respiratory diseases, poor blood circulation, liver trouble, exhaustion and weakness, and to boost qi, or life energy. It was also believed to prevent premature ageing.

The Japanese cultivated the mushroom by slicing Shii trees with axes and placing the logs by trees which were already growing Shiitake or contained Shiitake mushroom spores. Before 1982 the Japanese variety of these mushrooms could only be grown in traditional locations using ancient methods. In the late 1970s, Gary F. Leatham published a doctoral thesis based on his research on the budding and growth of the Japan Islands variety; the work helped make commercial cultivation possible worldwide, and Dr. Leatham is now known in the industry as the "Father of Shiitake farming in the USA".

Fresh and dried shiitake have many uses in the cuisines of East Asia. In Chinese cuisine, they are often sauteed in vegetarian dishes such as Buddha's delight. In Japan, they are served in miso soup, used as the basis for a kind of vegetarian dashi, and also as an ingredient in many steamed and simmered dishes. In Thailand, they may be served either fried or steamed.

Shiitake are often dried and sold as preserved food in packages. These must be rehydrated by soaking in water before using. Many people prefer dried shiitake to fresh, considering that the sun-drying process draws out the umami flavour from the dried mushrooms by breaking down proteins into amino acids and transforms ergosterol to vitamin D. The stems of shiitake are rarely used in Japanese and other cuisines, primarily because the stems are harder and take longer to cook than the soft fleshy caps. The highest grade of shiitake are called donko in Japanese.

Medicinal uses and scientific research

Research has demonstrated the Shiitake mushroom stimulates the immune system, contains a cholesterol lowering compound known as eritadenine, possesses anti-bacterial properties, possesses anti-viral properties (including anti-HIV and anti-HSV-1, contains a proteinase inhibitor) and reduces platelet aggregation

Active Hexose Correlated Compound (AHCC) is an alpha-glucan rich compound isolated from Shiitake. AHCC is a well tolerated compound that possesses antioxidant activity, and is metabolised via the CYP450 2D6 pathway. Research has indicated AHCC possesses the following activity.

 * Increasing resistance to pathogens in vivo (influenza virus, west Nile encephalitis, bacterial infection, various infectious agents, bacterial infection and influenza virus)
 * Producing an anti-cancer effect (on 269 human hepatocellular carcinoma patients and 44 hepatocellular carcinoma patients)
 * Enhancing immune function (double-blind, placebo-controlled trial of 21 people)

Lentinan, a compound isolated from Shiitake, is used as an intravenous anti-cancer agent in some countries. Lentinan was developed by the Japanese pharmaceutical company Ajinomoto, and designed to treat cancers of the stomach. Studies have demonstrated lentinan possesses anti-tumour properties and human clinical studies have associated lentinan with a higher survival rate, higher quality of life, and lower re-occurrence of cancer. Clinical research with lentinan includes studies with, 78 hepatocellular carcinoma patients, 32 gastric cancer patients, a multi-institutional study of lentinan and gastric cancer, a meta-analysis of lentinan and gastric cancer, 80 colorectal cancer patients, 20 gastric cancer patients, 36 hepatocellular carcinoma patients, and 29 pancreatic cancer patients. The City of Hope National Medical Center is currently conducting clinical trials to determine if a select portion of the Shiitake mushroom, which includes lentinan, can inhibit lung cancer.

11) **Coriolus** (*Trametes versicolour*)

Formerly known as Coriolus versicolour and Polyporus versicolour — Coriolus is an extremely common polypore mushroom which can be found throughout the world. Versicolour means 'of several colours' and it is true that this mushroom is found in a wide variety of different colours. T. versicolour is recognized as a medicinal mushroom in Chinese medicine under the name Yun Zhi and called Turkey Tail as a common name in western countries. In China and Japan T. versicolour is used as in immunoadjuvant therapy for cancer.

Coriolus has bioremediation potential as, according to world famous mycologist Paul Stamets, T. versicolour biodegrades a variety of pollutants.

Coriolus – *Trametes versicolour*

History

Coriolus versicolour is unique among the medicinal mushrooms, with extensive use in both traditional herbalism and modern clinical practice.

The focus of the modern clinical use and research (over 400 published studies), has been the immuno-modulating and anti-tumour properties of the hot water extracted polysaccharides. Originally isolated from the fruiting body (the mushroom), sales for these unique, all-natural compounds have reached several hundred million dollars a year in Japan and China, making them the most widely used products in those countries by people facing serious immune challenges

In classical Chinese and Japanese herbalism the fruit bodies (mushrooms) are harvested, dried, ground to a powder and made into tea. Given the extraction rate of the polysaccharides in a simple hot water extract (tea), it is interesting to note that the dose for the active compounds is the same in both traditional medicine and modern clinical practice.

In traditional herbalism hot water extracts of Coriolus were used to dispel dampness, reduce phlegm, treat pulmonary infections, and to support liver health. The Ming dynasty edition of the Materia Medica states "The black and green Yun zhi are beneficial to one's spirit and vital energy, and strengthen one's tendon and bone. If Yun zhi is taken for a long time, it will make one vigourous and live long." In Japan these mushrooms are also highly prized and sought after by people suffering from a variety of cancers. It was this popularity as a "folk remedy" that first got the attention of modern researchers.

Based on its reputation for healing within their traditional herbal practices Chinese and Japanese scientists began to do controlled clinical research on concentrated hot water extracts from Coriolus, studying the same 1-4, 1-3 polysaccharides (beta glucans) that would have been released into solution when making the hot water teas described in the texts from traditional Japanese and Chinese herbalism.

After placebo controlled clinical research demonstrated significant immuno-modulating properties the Coriolus 1-4, 1-3 polysaccharides (beta glucans) were approved as a pharmaceutical product by the Japanese Health Ministry, allowing health insurance to cover the cost of it's use.

At this point the Coriolus extract began to get widespread use by Japanese oncologists. Coriolus polysaccharides were used in practice to support immune health after surgical treatment for various conditions and to support and protect immune health in those patients receiving therapies where immune suppression is a prominent feature. Private and government sponsored research continued to monitor the effectiveness of the highly concentrated Coriolus extract in placebo controlled multi-institutional clinical studies, with the clinical evidence demonstrating significant immune benefit from daily use.

The Coriolus extract was so successful that the cost to Japan's national health insurance program reached almost a billion dollars a year. In an attempt to reduce expenditures the Health Ministry restricted the use of the Coriolus extract to those people most in need, people receiving chemotherapy or radiation. Clinical research has consistently demonstrated the ability of Coriolus beta glucans to double and even triple survival rates for people receiving chemotherapy and radiation.

Medicinal uses and scientific research

Coriolus versicolour, contains large quantities of Beta-glucans that act to stimulate the immune system. Coriolus can dramatically regenerate and rejuvenate the body. Its most active medicinal components are biological response modifiers called protein-bound polysaccharides. These polysaccharides are known as Krestin or PSK in Japan, and as Yun zhi, or PSP in China. There have been reports of cases of Bell's palsy clearing up with use of Coriolus for just a few days. Others have found it effective against bronchitis.

Coriolus versicolour has also been found to modulate autoimmune diseases and to be effective against human papillomavirus (HPV).

Coriolus is first line defense against infection. It is a good centerpiece for your natural medicine chest, even if you are currently the picture of health. When any type of infection strikes, you will be ready. Coriolus can be used to target any infected organ, gland or tissue. Its immune enhancing properties provide an increased response to deal effectively with infections, and do this without over stimulating the immune system.

Polysaccharide-K (Krestin, PSK), is a protein-bound polysaccharide isolated from Trametes versicolour, which is used as an immune system boosting agent in the treatment of cancer in some European countries as well as China and Japan. In Japan, PSK is approved as an adjuvant for cancer therapy and is covered by government health insurance.

PSK has documented anticancer activity in vitro, in vivo and in human clinical trials. Research has also demonstrated that the PSK can reduce mutagen-induced, radiation-induced, and spontaneously-induced cancer development. PSK has shown to be beneficial as an adjuvant in the treatment of gastric, oesophageal, colorectal, breast and lung cancers. Human clinical trials suggest PSK can reduce cancer recurrence when used as an adjuvant and research has demonstrated the mushroom can inhibit certain human cancer cell lines in vitro.

The United State's top ranked cancer hospital, the MD Anderson has reported that it is a "promising candidate for chemoprevention due to the multiple effects on the malignant process, limited side effects and safety of daily oral doses for extended periods of time."

Researchers at the Sloan-Kettering Cancer Center in New York tested several botanicals for their immune enhancing activity using a subcutaneous immunisation model of cell surface carbohydrate expression in cancer cells in a study published in September, 2008 Vaccine. They found Coriolus versicolour to display consistent and significant immune enhancement activity superior to all other compounds tested. The superiority of Coriolus to yeast beta-glucan, maitake, turmeric, echinacea, and preparation H-48 from Honso USA, was described as surprising. Although the exhibited levels of immune enhancing ability of astragalus was also impressive, it was surpassed by that of Coriolus.

The March, 2008 BMC Cancer reports Coriolus versicolour has shown anticancer activity with positive results in the treatment of gastric, oesophageal, colorectal, breast and lung cancers. The efficacy of its protein-bound polysaccharide as an immunomodulator is credited. This activity was independent of its previously described immunomodulatory effect on NK cells.

The journal Cancer Immunology and Immunotherapy reports double blind trials on 111 patients with colorectal cancer, using Coriolus versicolour. Although traditional medicine offers little help for colon cancer patients, Coriolus showed a remarkable enhancement of the patient's white blood cells, even in advanced colon cancer cases. The white cells greatly increased natural chemotactic motion and phagocytosis, the ability to scavenge toxins and kill pathogens. Coriolus was also used with patients as a helpful maintenance therapy following cancer surgery.

The results of a year long clinical trial examining the effects of mushroom supplementation in patients with Human Papillomavirus (HPV) were so impressive they were presented in 2008 at the 20th European Congress of Obstetrics and Gynocology. Dr. Silva Couto and his research team found that Coriolus versicolour supplementation over the period of one year substantially increased regression of dysplasia and induced clearance of the high-risk subtypes of the HPV responsible for cervical cancer. Coriolus supplementation demonstrated a 72 percent regression rate in lesions compared to 47.5 percent without supplementation, and a 90 percent regression rate in the high risk HPV virus sub-types compared to 8.5 percent without.

After using the supplement for one year, 72.5 percent of recipients reverted to normal cytology compared with only 47.5 percent of the control group. Coriolus supplementation produced a 90 percent regression rate in the high risk HPV virus sub-tupes compared to an 8.5 percent regression without supplementation.

It is also likely that Coriolus versicolour would be beneficial in high-grade squamous intraepithelial lesion (HSIL), a precancerous condition in which the cells of the uterine cervix are moderately or severely abnormal. The lead physician of the study noted that the optimal supplementation period may be as short as six months.

T cells belong to a group of while blood cells known as lymphocytes, and play a central role in cell-mediated immunity. The activation of T helper (Th) cell subsets also plays an important role in immunity. Uncontrolled Th responses lead to autoimmune and inflammatory diseases. The identification of agents that modulate these helper cells is essential for controlling autoimmune diseases. A study from the November, 2008 Journal of Pharmacy and Pharmacology, reported that polysaccharopeptide (PSP) from Coriolus versicolour exhibited the ability to control aberrant T lymphocyte activation through ciclosporin-like activity. PSP alone suppress production of activated T cells.

Coriolus is a potent immune boosting mushroom giving long-term immune support for chronic conditions, especially viral and fatigue related. In diseases causing a fall in white blood cells, Dr Rotolo of Italy found that after supplementation with 30 grammes of Coriolus per day, white cells were increased by 27% within 15 days. Dr Munro of London found that there was an increase in natural killer cells activity.

Other studies have shown that Coriolus can double the number of natural killer cells after only 8 weeks of treatment. Coriolus has also been found to help patients with chronic fatigue syndrome and may be an effective treatment for Lyme disease.

Japanese researchers screened 200 of the best phytochemicals (plant extracts) known for anti-tumour activity. Coriolus versicolour was designated as exhibiting the greatest amount of anti-tumour activity. In another Japanese study, 185 people with lung cancer at different stages were given radiation. Doctors found those who also took Coriolus showed the best tumour shrinkage and the best survival rate. Another study involving stomach cancer patients produced similar results. Those who received Coriolus survived significantly longer, felt better and had fewer side effects.

12) Agaricus Blazei Murill

Agaricus Blazei Murill (also known as ABM and sometimes Agaricus subrufescens although the latter name has not yet been established, see below) is a species of mushroom, sometimes known as "Himematsutake" and by a number of other names. This Agaricus is a choice edible, with a somewhat sweet taste and fragrance of almonds. The almond flavour is due to the presence of benzaldehyde, benzyl alcohol, benzonitrile, and methyl benzoate. This mushroom is also well known for its purported medicinal properties.

History

ABM was first described by the American botanist Charles Horton Peck in 1893. During the late 19th and early 20th century, it was cultivated for the table in the eastern United States. It was discovered again in Brazil during the 1970s, and thought to be a new species, Agaricus subrufescens.

Agaricus Blazei Murill

In 2002, Didukh and Wasser rejected the name A. blazei and called the Brazilian fungi Agaricus brasiliensis; this was rejected by Kerrigan through genetic and interfertility testing on several fungal strains. Samples of the Brazilian strains called A. blazei and A. braziliensis proved to be genetically similar to, and interfertile with, the North American population of Agaricus subrufescens. These tests also found European samples called A. rufotegulis to be of the same species. Because Agaricus subrufescensis is the oldest name, it is traditionally considered the scientifically, historically correct name but this issue remains inconclusive.

Medicinal use and scientific research

Because of its high beta glucan content – higher than both Reishi and Shiitake mushrooms – ABM is used in oncological therapy, mainly in Japan and California. It has been commercially cultivated in Asia and South America since 1993. Because of this valuable polysaccharide, and lack of supply, ABM used to be relatively expensive, until it was successfully artificially cultivated in mushroom farms in Asia and South America for over 15 years for the health food market. China (Maucua) and Brazil are major exporters.

Recently, Watanabe et al. published a report in the Biological & Pharmaceutical Bulletin on a novel hybrid of the ABM called Basidiomycetes-X (BDM-X) and a US patent was issued on a novel hybrid of the ABM edible mushroom which was cross-bred (hybridized) with another medicinal mushroom resulting in a new hybrid claimed to possess 10 to 3000 times the potency of similar but unpatented mushrooms.

Over 100 clinical trials and citations on Medline suggest that the ABM mushroom possesses unique anti-oxidant and ant-proliferative effects that are being studied in the treatment of cancer and diseases of the liver.

ABM mushroom specifically assists in the production of interferon and interleukin, which are potent in fighting off cancer cell metastasis, especially cancer of the uterus. It also reduces blood glucose, blood pressure, cholesterol levels and the effects of arteriosclerosis. It is used traditionally against a range of diseases, including chronic hepatitis and has recently been shown to have strong immunomodulating properties, which has led to increasing scientific interest. Some novel findings from the University of Oslo, Norway, point to highly different biological potency between AbM extracts of different source and manufacturing. Also a study from the Qiqihar Medical College in China, found that a low molecular weight polysaccharide isolated from ABM suppresses tumour growth and angiogenesis in vivo.

ABM is known to contain three different beta-glucans – beta-(1-3)-D-glucan, beta-(1-4)-alpha-D-glucan, and beta-(1-6)-D-glucan. Most researchers believe that betaglucans, a plant polysaccharide, are the primary immune enhancing factor in the mushroom.

13) **Olive leaf** (*Olea europaea*)

Olive leaf is the leaf of the olive tree which is a small evergreen tree native to Mediterranean regions, but naturalised to climates as varied as those of Australia, California, and Texas. The well-known green to blue-black fruit of this tree yields a useful, edible oil. Both the oil and the dried green-greyish coloured leaves are used in herbal medicine.

Recorded evidence of olive leaf's medicinal use dates back thousands of years as it was used by ancient Egyptian and Mediterranean cultures to treat a variety of health conditions. Olive leaf is the first botanical cited in the Bible (Ezekiel 47:12) as a natural healer: "The fruit thereof shall be for meat, and the leaf thereof for medicine."

The primary medical constituents contained in unprocessed olive leaf are believed to be the antioxidant oleuropein and hydroxytyrosol, as well as several other polyphenols and flavonoids including Oleocanthal.

Olive leaves and fruit

Medicinal use and scientific research

Olive leaf and extracts are utilised in the complementary and alternative medicine community for its ability to act as a natural pathogens killer by inhibiting the replication process of many pathogens. Olive leaf is commonly used to fight colds and flu, yeast infections, and viral infections such as the hard-to-treat Epstein-Barr disease, shingles and herpes. Olive leaf is also good for the heart and has shown to reduce low-density lipoproteins (LDL), or bad cholesterol.

One of the most active chemicals found in the leaves of olive trees is known as oleuropein. In a few small human studies, oleuropein has reduced existing high blood pressure. In one study, 40 pairs of twins at the upper limit of normal blood pressure were divided into groups so that one twin took olive leaf extract and the other twin received no medication. After eight weeks, blood pressure generally decreased for individuals taking 1000 mg per day of olive leaf extract. Blood pressure remained at higher levels for those taking a smaller dose of olive leaf extract or no medication. Results of more extensive animal studies suggest that it may also prevent or lessen the development of high blood pressure. Several of oleuropein's actions may be responsible for olive leaf extract's effects on blood pressure. First, oleuropein is thought to relax blood vessels. The heart does not have to pump with as much force and blood pressure goes down. Oleuropein may also prevent deposits of cholesterol in the arteries. In addition, in one small study of healthy humans, it reduced the stickiness of blood components known as platelets. Both cholesterol and platelets can build up in arteries to form plaques, causing arteriosclerosis or "hardening of the arteries". More studies are needed to confirm or deny these effects.

In other studies, olive leaf extract and oleuropein have lowered blood sugar levels in laboratory animals with diabetes. It is believed that they have a dual effect-- causing more glucose to be utilised by the body and also stimulating the release of insulin. Few results are available from human studies, however; and many of the animal studies used injectable forms of olive leaf extract that are not commonly available for human use.

In recently reported laboratory studies, oral extracts of olive leaf have shown anti- infective properties. Extracts are concentrated liquid preparations usually made by soaking chopped or mashed plant parts in a liquid such as alcohol, and then straining out the solid parts. In separate studies, contact with olive leaf extract killed specific types of bacteria and slowed the growth of some skin fungi and interfered with some of the infective properties of HIV, the virus that causes AIDS. Other laboratory studies found that an extract of olive leaf may stop the growth of cancer cells. Much more study in animals and humans is needed to confirm or disprove the potential anti-infective and anticancer effects of olive leaf extract, however.

In a recent small study, oleuropein was tested as a topical preparation. Volunteers applied either a gel or a cream-like formulation to skin before being exposed to ultraviolet light. Individuals using the olive-derived products had less dryness and reddening than those who used products that did not contain oleuropein. Although much more research is needed, oleuropein may become an additive for cosmetics.

14) **Black Cumin** (*Nigella sativa*)

Nigella sativa is an annual flowering plant, native to southwest Asia. It grows to 20–30 cm tall, with finely divided, linear (but not thread-like) leaves. The flowers are delicate, and usually coloured pale blue and white, with 5–10 petals. The fruit is a large and inflated capsule composed of 3–7 united follicles, each containing numerous seeds. The seed is used as a spice.

In English, Nigella sativa seed is variously called Black cumin, fennel flower, nutmeg flower, Roman coriander, blackseed, black caraway, or black onion seed. Other names used, sometimes misleadingly, are onion seed and black sesame, both of which are similar-looking but unrelated. The seeds are frequently referred to as black cumin, but this is also used for a different spice, Bunium persicum. The scientific name is a derivative of Latin niger "black". An older English name gith is now used for the corncockle.

Nigella sativa has a pungent bitter taste and a faint smell of strawberries. It is used primarily in candies and liquors. The variety of naan bread called Peshawari naan is as a rule topped with kalonji seeds. In herbal medicine, Nigella sativa has anti-hypertensive, carminative, and anthelminthic properties. They are eaten by elephants to aid digestion.

Black Cumin flower

History

According to Zohary and Hopf, archeological evidence about the earliest cultivation of N. sativa "is still scanty", but they report that N. sativa seeds have been found in several sites from ancient Egypt, including Tutenkhamen's tomb. Although its exact role in Egyptian culture is unknown, it is known that items entombed with a pharaoh were carefully selected to assist him in the after life.

The earliest written reference to N. sativa is thought to be in the book of Isaiah in the Old Testament where the reaping of nigella and wheat is contrasted (Isaiah 28: 25, 27). Easton's Bible dictionary states that the Hebrew word ketsah refers to without doubt to N. sativa (although not all translations are in agreement). According to Zohary and Hopf, N. sativa "was another traditional condiment of the Old World during classical times; and its black seeds were extensively used to flavour food."

Medicinal use and scientific research

Nigella sativa has been used for medicinal purposes for centuries, both as a herb and pressed into oil, in Asia, Middle East, and Africa. It has been traditionally used for a variety of conditions and treatments related to respiratory health, stomach and intestinal health, kidney and liver function, circulatory and immune system support, and for general well-being.

In Islam, it is regarded as one of the greatest forms of healing medicine available. Prophet Muhammad once stated that the black seed can heal every disease - except death.

The seeds have been traditionally used in the Middle East and Southeast Asian countries to treat ailments including asthma, bronchitis, rheumatism and related inflammatory diseases, to increase milk production in nursing mothers, to promote digestion and to fight parasitic infections. Its oil has been used to treat skin conditions such as eczema and boils and to treat cold symptoms. Its many uses have earned nigella the Arabic approbation 'Habbatul barakah', meaning the seed of blessing.

Black cumin oil contains nigellone, which protects guinea pigs from histamine-induced bronchial spasms (perhaps explaining its use to relieve the symptoms of asthma, bronchitis, and coughing). The presence of an anti-tumour sterol, beta sitosterol, lends credence to its traditional use to treat abscesses and tumours of the abdomen, eyes, and liver. Nigella Sativa oil is also known to have opioid agonistic properties.

A study by Ali BH. and Blunden G. from King Saud University of Saudi Arabia, found that treatment of rats with the seed extract for up to 12 weeks has been reported to induce changes in the haemogram that include an increase in both the packed cell volume (PCV) and haemoglobin (Hb), and a decrease in plasma concentrations of cholesterol, triglycerides and glucose. The seeds are characterized by a very low degree of toxicity. It would appear that the beneficial effects of the use of the seeds and thymoquinone might be related to their cytoprotective and antioxidant actions, and to their effect on some mediators of inflammation.

Anti-parasitic and anticestodal effects of N. sativa seeds were studied in children naturally infected with the respective worm. A single oral administration of 40 mg/kg of N. sativa seeds and equivalent amount of its ethanolic extract were effective in reducing the egg count in the faeces, with a comparable effect to niclosamide. The crude extracts also did not produce any adverse side effects from all the doses tested.

In 2007, Abdulelah and Zainal-Abidin investigated the anti-malarial activities of different extracts of N.sativa seeds against P. berghei. Results indicated strong biocidal effects against the parasite.

Researchers at the Kimmel Cancer at Jefferson in Philadelphia have found that thymoquinone, an extract of nigella sativa seed oil, blocked pancreatic cancer cell growth and killed the cells by enhancing the process of programmed cell death, (apoptosis). While the studies are in the early stages, the findings suggest that thymoquinone could eventually have some use as a preventative strategy in patients who have gone through surgery and chemotherapy or in individuals who are at a high risk of developing cancer.

15) **Turmeric** (*Curcuma longa*)

Turmeric (Curcuma longa) is a rhizomatous herbaceous perennial plant of the ginger family, Zingiberaceae which is native to tropical South Asia. It needs temperatures between 20° C and 30° C, and a considerable amount of annual rainfall to thrive. Plants are gathered annually for their rhizomes, and re-seeded from some of those rhizomes in the following season. It is often misspelled (or pronounced) as tumeric. In medieval Europe, turmeric became known as Indian Saffron, since it is widely used as an alternative to far more expensive saffron spice.

Its rhizomes are boiled for several hours and then dried in hot ovens, after which they are ground into a deep orange-yellow powder commonly used as a spice in curries and other South Asian and Middle Eastern cuisine, for dyeing, and to impart colour to mustard condiments. Its active ingredient is curcumin and it has an earthy, bitter, peppery flavour and a mustardy smell.

Turmeric contains up to 5% essential oils and up to 3% curcumin, a polyphenol. It is the active substance of turmeric and it is also known as C.I. 75300, or Natural Yellow 3. The systematic chemical name is (1E,6E)-1,7-bis(4-hydroxy-3-methoxyphenyl)-1,6-heptadiene-3,5-dione.

A representation of the various parts of Turmeric in a herbal compendium

Medicinal uses and scientific research

In Ayurvedic medicine, turmeric is thought to have many medicinal properties and many in India use it as a readily available antiseptic for cuts, burns, bruises and it is also used as an antibacterial agent. It is taken in some Asian countries as a dietary supplement, which allegedly helps with stomach problems and other ailments and it is popular as a tea in Okinawa, Japan.

Turmeric is known to be a strong antioxidant, a substance thought to protect body cells from damage caused by a chemical process called oxidation. The chemical breakdown of foods into components the body can use, oxidation also produces by-products. Known as oxygen free radicals, some by-products of oxidation may suppress immune function and cause tissue damage. In addition to their anticancer effects, antioxidants in turmeric may protect the brain, kidneys, liver, and lungs from damage by alcohol, drugs, radiation, heavy metals such as lead, or chemicals such as dry cleaning fluid. Some laboratory research seems to show that curcumin may also help to lessen some of the complications of cancer, particularly a reduction in the amount of bone in the body.

Recently, curcumin – an active ingredient and antioxidant in Turmeric - has received a great deal more attention in studies than turmeric as a whole herb. Researchers are studying curcumin to learn whether it is an effective anti-inflammatory agent and whether it holds any promise as a cancer drug. It is currently being investigated for possible benefits in Alzheimer's disease, cancer and liver disorders as it is only in recent years that Western scientists have increasingly recognised the medicinal properties of turmeric. According to a 2005 article in the Wall Street Journal titled, "Common Indian Spice Stirs Hope," research activity into curcumin, the active ingredient in turmeric, is exploding. In that year supplement sales increased 35% from 2004, and the U.S. National Institutes of Health had four clinical trials underway to study curcumin treatment for pancreatic cancer, multiple myeloma, Alzheimer's, and colorectal cancer.

A 2004 UCLA-Veterans Affairs study involving genetically altered mice suggests that curcumin, the active ingredient in turmeric, might inhibit the accumulation of destructive beta amyloids in the brains of Alzheimer's disease patients and also break up existing plaques. "Curcumin has been used for thousands of years as a safe anti-inflammatory in a variety of ailments as part of Indian traditional medicine," Gregory Cole, Professor of medicine and neurology at the David Geffen School of Medicine at UCLA said.

Curcumin has been identified as a powerful MAO-A inhibitor, at doses above 150 mg/kg. MAO-B inhibition was not present until doses escalate above 550mg/kg.

Another 2004 study conducted at Yale University involved oral administration of curcumin to mice homozygous for the most common allele implicated in cystic fibrosis. Treatment with curcumin restored physiologically-relevant levels of protein function. Anti-tumoural effects against melanoma cells have also been demonstrated and a recent study involving mice has shown that turmeric slows the spread of breast cancer into lungs and other body parts. Turmeric also enhances the effect of taxol in reducing metastasis of breast cancer.

According to a review article published by researchers from the Ohio State University in Columbus, curcumin demonstrated anti-cancer effects at virtually all stages of tumour development in rodents. It showed potential to kill cancer cells and prevent normal cells from becoming cancerous. A French laboratory study concluded that curcumin appeared to be a potent inhibitor of cancer development and several more laboratory studies also concluded that curcumin might prevent and slow the growth of some types of tumour cells. Animal studies in the United Kingdom suggested that curcumin slows the growth of adenomas in the intestine in mice and a recent United States mouse study also showed that it slowed the spread of breast cancer to the lungs.

In promising but very early results from laboratory, animal, and human studies, curcumin has kept several kinds of cancers from starting, growing, or spreading. Curcumin may speed up the rate at which certain kinds of cancer cells die by damaging cancer cell DNA. It may disrupt the formation of microtubules to interfere with cancer cell division, and it may also prevent the growth of blood vessels that support tumour growth. Since it is not well absorbed from the intestines, turmeric may reach high enough levels to be especially active for cancers of the colon and other intestinal conditions, such as Crohn's disease. Additionally, in a few preliminary laboratory studies of human cancer cells, curcumin has shown possible ability to make cancer cells more susceptible to radiation therapy. It may increase the anticancer effects of certain medications, as well.

Curcumin is also thought to be an antinociceptive agent (pain reliever). In the November 2006 issue of Arthritis & Rheumatism, a study was published that showed the effectiveness of turmeric in the reduction of joint inflammation, and recommended clinical trials as a possible treatment for the alleviation of arthritis symptoms. It is thought to work as a natural inhibitor of the COX-2 enzyme, and has been shown effective in animal models for neuropathic pain secondary to diabetes, among others.

In recent studies, curcumin (also known as diferuloylmethane)--one of the active chemicals contained in turmeric--has been found to limit the activity of several chemicals including two enzymes, lipoxygenase (LOX) and cyclooxygenase-2 (COX-2), that are involved in promoting and maintaining inflammation. By reducing the effects of these enzymes, curcumin may also reduce inflammation and the pain associated with it.

Presenting their findings at the Endocrine Society's annual meeting in San Francisco in June 2008, researchers discovered that turmeric-treated mice were less susceptible to developing type 2 diabetes, based on their blood glucose levels, and glucose and insulin tolerance tests. They also discovered that turmeric-fed obese mice showed significantly reduced inflammation in fat tissue and liver compared to controls. They speculate that curcumin in the turmeric lessens insulin resistance and prevents type 2 diabetes in these mouse models by dampening the inflammatory response provoked by obesity.

Curcumin is being studied to see if it helps other diseases as well. One small study of curcumin, along with another antioxidant called quercetin, was done in adults who received kidney transplants. Those who received the combination in high dosages had fewer transplant rejections than those who received lower doses or placebo. Curcumin may also promote the emptying of the gallbladder, and seemed to help prevent stomach ulcers in rodents. Early research has suggested that curcumin may help lower "bad cholesterol," reduce inflammation, and help with arthritis symptoms, although more reliable human studies are still needed and in studies of mice, curcumin appeared to help with blocking the plaques and proteins that cause problems in the brain during Alzheimer Disease.

In laboratory and animal studies, chemicals in turmeric have appeared to affect several of the pathways that are thought to cause accumulation of the proteins associated with Alzheimer's disease. A small cohort study of Asian individuals between 60 years old and 93 years old found less cognitive disability in those who regularly ate foods containing turmeric. Cognition is the ability to think, learn, understand, imagine, reason, and remember.

16) **Liquorice** (*Glycyrrhiza glabra*)

The liquorice plant is a legume (related to beans and peas) and native to southern Europe and parts of Asia. It grows best in deep, fertile, well-drained soils, with full sun, and is harvested in the autumn two to three years after planting. Dried liquorice root can be chewed as a sweet. Liquorice extract is produced by boiling liquorice root and subsequently evaporating most of the water. In fact, the name 'liquorice'/'licorice' is derived (via the Old French licoresse), from the Ancient Greek glukurrhiza, meaning 'sweet root'. Liquorice extract is traded both in solid and syrup form. Its active principle is glycyrrhizin, a sweetener more than 50 times as sweet as sucrose which also has pharmaceutical effects.

Liquorice is popular in Italy (particularly in the South) and Spain in its natural form. The root of the plant is simply dug up, washed and chewed as mouth-freshener. Throughout Italy unsweetened liquorice is consumed in the form of small black pieces made only from 100% pure liquorice extract; the taste is bitter and intense. In Calabria a popular liqueur is made from pure liquorice extract and liquorice is also very popular in Syria where it is sold as a drink. It is also the main ingredient of a very well known soft drink in Egypt, called 'erk-soos. Chinese cuisine uses liquorice as a culinary spice for savoury foods, it is often employed to flavour broths and foods simmered in soy sauce. Other herbs and spices of similar flavour include anise, star anise, tarragon, and fennel.

Medicinal use and scientific research

Liquorice has been used in ancient Greece, China, and Egypt, primarily for gastritis (inflammation of the stomach) and ailments of the upper respiratory tract. Ancient Egyptians prepared a liquorice drink for ritual use to honour spirits of the pharaohs. Its use became widespread in Europe and Asia for numerous indications and has become one of the most widely used herbs worldwide.

In traditional Chinese medicine, liquorice is used in over 5000 herbal formulae to "harmonise" the other ingredients in the formula, to carry the formula into all 12 of the regular meridians and to relieve a spasmodic cough.

About 8% of the liquorice plant is made up of a glycoside called glycyrrhizin. Chemicals that contain both sugar and non-sugar components, glycosides may have many effects in the body. In addition to giving liquorice its sweet taste, glycyrrhizin specifically reduces the activity of two enzymes that break down prostaglandin E (PGE). Low levels of PGE are associated with stomach conditions such as colic, stomach inflammation, and ulcers. By interfering with the body's removal of PGE, glycyrrhizin allows more PGE to circulate in the blood. The resulting increased levels of PGE may increase the production of stomach mucus and decrease the production of stomach acid. Both effects help to protect stomach tissue, so liquorice has been used to treat ulcers and other stomach conditions.

In oriental countries, chronic hepatitis and other liver conditions traditionally have been treated with liquorice. Its anti-inflammatory effects help to preserve liver function, and liquorice may also help keep hepatitis viruses from becoming established in liver tissue. Glycyrrhizin seems to enhance the activity of some prescription drugs for hepatitis. Additionally, glycyrrhizin appears to decrease the effects of certain enzymes that are involved with liver damage, so it may be used in combination with certain cancer drugs that are known to cause liver damage. Enzymes are body proteins that accelerate or regulate biological processes.

Glycyrrhizin also encourages the formation of mucus in the respiratory tract. This increase may make respiratory tract mucus less sticky and may also promote its elimination from the body. In addition, very sweet substances such as liquorice are known to enhance the elimination of mucus from the lungs. Therefore, liquorice has been used to treat respiratory conditions such as bronchitis. It may also be used to soothe a sore throat. Because other chemicals in liquorice are known to suppress coughing, it may be included in cough syrups and cough lozenges as both a cough suppressant and a flavouring. Powdered liquorice root is an effective expectorant, and has been used for this purpose since ancient times, especially in Ayurvedic medicine where it is also used in tooth powders and is known as Jastimadhu. Modern cough syrups often include liquorice extract as an ingredient.

Liquorice also shows some anti-infective and anticancer properties. In laboratory and animal studies, liquorice and chemicals contained in it have stopped or slowed the growth of certain bacteria, fungi, and parasites. Several animal studies have also revealed a possibly strong antiviral effect for liquorice. In many studies, liquorice components that belong to the isoflavonoid class of chemicals appeared to have several anti-infective effects that include interference with oxygen utilisation by infective micro-organisms. Chemicals derived from liquorice have shown anticancer activity in animal studies and in laboratory cultures of human cancer cells.

As reported by the American Cancer Society, these studies have identified several substances found in liquorice that may help prevent DNA mutations, inhibit tumour formation, or even kill cancer cells. For example, Licochalcone-A, glabridin, and licocoumarone have been tested using cancer cells growing in laboratory dishes, and preliminary studies indicate that these chemicals can cause breast cancer, prostate cancer, and leukaemia cells to stop growing or even to die.

Glycyrrhizin and glycyrrhizic acid reduced formation of skin, colon, liver, and breast cancers in mice. Glycyrrhizin may be useful as a treatment for chronic hepatitis, and a Japanese study found that patients with chronic hepatitis C who took this supplement were less likely to develop liver cancer. This study asked patients to remember and report whether they had used the supplement in the past (retrospective.) This kind of study is considered less reliable than a clinical trial that randomly assigns patients to various treatments and then follows them over time to find out what happens.

Additionally, liquorice may have some ability to improve functioning of the immune system. Early studies suggest that glycyrrhizin may inhibit HIV replication in patients with AIDS. It is an adaptogen which helps reregulate the hypothalamic-pituitary-adrenal axis and can also be used for auto-immune conditions including lupus, scleroderma, rheumatoid arthritis and animal dander allergies.

Liquorice is also thought to have mild influences on sex hormones. It may either increase or decrease natural amounts of the female hormone, oestrogen. Animal studies show that high doses of liquorice may prevent oestrogen from attaching to oestrogen receptors, thereby reducing oestrogen's effects. In other studies, liquorice seemed to speed up the body's breakdown of oestrogen, but only if blood levels of oestrogen were already low. If oestrogen levels were high, liquorice appeared to have the opposite effect. Taking liquorice may also alter testosterone levels in men.

Dried Liquorice roots

For topical use, liquorice or its components may be included in shampoos to reduce scalp oil or in products to relieve irritated skin. In studies, a topical gel containing 2% of glycyrrhizin reduced itching, redness, and swelling from dermatitis. A non-prescription patch containing liquorice root has been shown in studies to ease the pain and promote the healing of aphthous ulcers (canker sores) better than placebo (an identical but inactive patch) or no treatment at all. Liquorice is also a mild laxative and may be used as a topical antiviral agent for shingles, ophthalmic, oral or genital herpes.

The compounded carbenoxolone is derived from liquorice. Studies indicate it may inhibit an enzyme in the brain that is involved in making stress-related hormones, which have been associated with age-related mental decline.

17) **Chaga** (*Inonotus obliquus*)

Chaga, also known as cinder conk, is a fungus in Hymenochaetaceae family. It is a parasitic fungus on Birch and other trees. The sterile conk is irregularly formed and has the appearance of burnt charcoal. The fertile fruitbody can be found very rarely as a resupinate (crustose) fungus on or near the clinker, usually appearing after the host tree is completely dead. I. obliquus grows in birch forests of Russia, Korea, Eastern Europe, Northern areas of the United States and in the North Carolina mountains. The Chaga mushroom is sold as a medicinal mushroom in the health supplement industry.

The superior grade of Chaga included in Theriaca Elixir is harvested only once every 20 years from selected birch trees.

Chaga mushroom on a birch tree

History

Chaga mushroom is somewhat different from most other medicinal mushrooms. This parasitic fungus grows on birch trees and eventually results in the death of its host. The outwards visible growth, also known as tinder conk for its use in igniting fire, is solid, black and crumbly, resembling a big lump of charcoal.

Since the 16th century, there are records of Chaga mushroom being used in folk medicine and the botanical medicine of the Eastern European countries as a remedy for cancer, gastritis, ulcers, and tuberculosis of the bones.[citation needed] In 1958, scientific studies in Finland and Russia found Chaga provided an epochal effect in breast cancer, liver cancer,uterine cancer, and gastric cancer, as well as in hypertension and diabetes. Herbalist David Winston maintains that it is the strongest anti-cancer medicinal mushroom.

Chaga was completely unknown in the western world, until Russian author and later Nobel laureate Alexandr Solzhenitsyn introduced it to the world in his novel Cancer Ward, whose protagonist is cured of cancer with the help of Chaga. Cancer Ward is thought to be autobiographical, as Solzhenitsyn suffered from cancer himself.

Besides cancer, in folk medicine Chaga mushroom has been used in the treatment of various stomach problems, tuberculosis, hypertension, viral infections, cardiovascular disease and diabetes. Recently it has attracted attention as a potential therapy for HIV infection.

Medicinal use and scientific research

The antimutagenic action of the molecules found in the white part of birch bark where Chaga feeds inhibits free-radical oxidation and also induces the production of interferons, which helps induce DNA repair. The substances, contained in white part of birch bark contribute to the decrease of hypoxia and to increase of the stability of organism to the oxygen deficiency, being antihypoxant correcting the metabolism of cells. The anti-cancer properties of betulin or betulinic acid, a chemical isolated from birch trees, is now being studied for use as a chemotherapeutic agent. Chaga contains large amounts of betulinic acid in a form that can be ingested orally, and it also contains the full spectrum of immune-stimulating phytochemicals found in other medicinal mushrooms such as maitake mushroom and shiitake mushroom.

In 1998 there was a study in Poland that demonstrated Chaga's inhibiting effects on tumour growth. Noda and colleagues found that betulin seems to work highly selectively on tumour cells because the interior pH of tumour tissues is generally lower than that of normal tissues, and betulinic acid is only active at those lower levels. Fulda et al. found in 1997 that once inside the cells, betulinic acid induces apoptosis (programmed cell death) in the tumours. In 2005, I. obliquus was evaluated for its potential for protecting against oxidative damage to DNA in human lymphocytes. The study found that the polyphenolic extract protected these cells against hydrogen peroxide-induced oxidative stress. Another study that year found the endo-polysaccharide of Chaga produced indirect anti-cancer effects via immuno-stimulation. The mycelial endo-polysaccharide of I. obliquus was identified as a candidate for use as an immune response modifier and indicate that the anti-cancer effect of endo-polysaccharide is not directly tumourcidal but rather is immuno-stimulating. It has also have anti-inflammatory properties. Saitoh Akiko published on the antimutagenic effects of Chaga in 1996, and Mizuno et al. published on the anti tumour and hypoglycemic activities of the polysaccharides from the sclerotia and mycelia of Chaga.

18) **Muscadine** (*Vitis rotundifolia*)

Muscadines are a grapevine species native to the present-day southeastern United States that has been extensively cultivated since the 16th Century. Its recognised range in the United States extends from New York south to Florida, and west to Missouri, Kansas, Arkansas, Oklahoma and Texas. They are well adapted to their native warm and humid climate; they need fewer chilling hours than better known varieties and they thrive on summer heat.

The muscadine berries range from bronze to dark purple to black in colour when ripe. They have skin sufficiently tough that eating the raw fruit often involves biting a small hole in the skin to suck out the pulp inside. Muscadines are not only eaten fresh, but also are used in making wine, juice, and jelly. A Mississippi State University nutritionist reported that a purée of muscadine skins and pulp is an excellent source also of dietary fibre, essential minerals and carbohydrates and is low in fat. Muscadine purée powder has more dietary fibre than oat or rice bran.

Muscadine grapes are rich sources of polyphenols and other nutrients studied for their potential health benefits. Reports have indicated that muscadine grapes may contain high concentrations of resveratrol — a polyphenol with reported beneficial health effects — and that wines produced from these grapes, both red and white, may contain more than 40 mg/L of resveratrol. However, subsequent studies have found no or little resveratrol in different varieties of muscadine grapes.

Medicinal uses and scientific research

As muscadine grapes are notable for their highly pigmented, thick skins in which the content of polyphenols is known to be high, research interest in describing these phytochemicals is significant.

Resveratrol is produced by many plants, apparently due to its antifungal properties. It is found in widely varying amounts in grapes (primarily the skins). Ordinary non-muscadine red wine contains between 0.2 and 5.8 mg/L, depending on the grape variety, while white wine has much less - the reason being that red wine is fermented with the skins, allowing the wine to absorb the resveratrol, whereas white wine is fermented after the skin has been removed. Wines produced from muscadine grapes, both red and white, may contain more than 40 mg/L.

In grapes, resveratrol is found primarily in the skin and seeds. This is particularly true for muscadine grapes, whose skin and seeds have been reported to have about one hundred times the concentration as the pulp. The amount found in grape skins also varies with the grape cultivar, its geographic origin, and exposure to fungal infection.

Several studies have detected substantial amounts of resveratrol in Muscadine berries and seeds. Concentrations for the berries without seeds have been reported to range from 3 to 24 ppm (parts per million) in dried samples. Containing an average of 43 ppm, the high seed concentration of resveratrol could be significant during muscadine wine making when the fermenting wine is in contact with seeds. Muscadine pomace, the solids left after pressing, contained 18 to 84 ppm in dried samples. A purée made from the pomace with the seeds removed contained 10 to 62 ppm. For juices, resveratrol was found in concentrations ranging from 3 to 13 mg/L.

Muscadine leaves and fruit

As one of nature's richest sources of polyphenolic antioxidants, muscadines have been studied for their potential health benefits which include preliminary evidence for effects against cancer mechanisms. To date, in vitro studies have shown positive effects of muscadine phenolics against blood, colon and prostate cancers. Polyphenols, (including the subclass of proanthocyanidins) are recognised to be effective antioxidants, substances thought to protect body cells from damage caused by a chemical process called oxidation, which produces oxygen free radicals; antioxidants are believed to work in a number of ways. They may lessen oxidation, they may inactivate oxygen free radicals, and they may restore at least some normal functioning to tissues damaged by oxygen free radicals.

For example, human case reports and results from some laboratory and animal studies appear to show that grape seed extract may help to prevent and treat heart diseases such as high blood pressure and high cholesterol. By limiting oxidation, antioxidants in grape seed extract may help prevent changes, including damage to blood vessels, that may contribute to the development of heart disease. In studies of animals with chemically induced diabetes, grape seed extract helped protect against heart damage from high blood sugar levels. Substances in grape seed extract may also block the effects of enzymes that process fats--including cholesterol--from the diet. Consequently, less fat may be absorbed and more may be eliminated from the body. In a long-term study of laboratory mice, a diet containing a compound found in grape seed extract was comparable to a calorie-restricted diet in maintaining heart function and preventing some of the health effects of ageing.

Proanthocyanidins are also believed to block the deterioration of blood vessels. Therefore, grape seed extract may improve conditions involving veins and arteries. It has been used to prevent, delay, and treat a condition known as chronic venous insufficiency, which occurs when valves in the veins that carry blood back to the heart are weak or damaged. The blood that collects in the veins of the legs as a result can lead to varicose veins, spider veins, or sores on the legs. Results that are more serious may include blood clots in the legs or sores that do not heal and may become infected. The possible blood vessel strengthening effect of grape seed extract may also help to prevent and treat haemorrhoids.

Since proanthocyanidins in grape seed extract strengthen the walls of all blood vessels, they may also help to keep damaged, stretched, or stiff blood vessels from leaking. In one area of research, grape seed extract has shown promise for slowing retinopathy, the gradual break down of the retinas in the eyes. A common contributor to retinopathy is damage to the small blood vessels in the eyes. Individuals with diabetes, arteriosclerosis (a build up of fatty deposits in the arteries), or other conditions that increase the likelihood for blood vessel damage are more likely to have serious vision problems as a result of that damage. Grape seed extract may also reduce eye stress caused by bright lights. In studies of laboratory animals, it has had some effectiveness for preventing cataract development and delaying the enlargement of existing cataracts, but further study is needed to determine whether grape seed extract improves human eye conditions.

One of the polyphenols contained in grape seed extract is called resveratrol. In laboratory and animal studies, resveratrol from grape seeds has interfered with cancer cell growth and division, as well as causing some cancer cells to disintegrate faster than they would ordinarily. In addition, it may also block enzymes that initiate and prolong the survival of several cancer cell types, including breast cancer, prostate cancer, and skin cancer. As a result, tumours may either stop growing or actually shrink because higher than usual numbers of cancer cells die. Some human case studies suggest that proanthocyanidins promote the body's release of certain immune system cells, including interleukin-12 (IL-12) and T-cells, to tumour tissue. All these possible effects mean resveratrol may have direct anticancer activity. It may also act indirectly by increasing the effectiveness, lowering the side effects, or both of many drugs currently used for cancer chemotherapy. One possible result is that taking resveratrol during chemotherapy may allow lower doses of cancer drugs to be effective. Reductions in doses may also reduce the potential for serious side effects from the cancer drugs.

Recently, a specific formulation of resveratrol known as SRT501 was given orphan-drug status by the U.S Food and Drug Administration (FDA). An orphan drug has received FDA approval because it shows effectiveness for treating severe or rare diseases that usually have few other treatment options. SRT501 is effective for treating MELAS syndrome, a rare inherited disorder that causes brain and muscle deterioration--usually in individuals under the age of 20 years old.

Effects similar to possible anticancer activity have been seen in laboratory studies of grape seed extract against viruses, including HIV, the virus that causes AIDS. Although the exact ways that grape seed extract may fight HIV and other viruses are not known, it is thought that grape seed extract interferes with viral multiplication, possibly by preventing viral attachment to host cells. How high doses of resveratrol and other chemicals in grape seed extract may affect normal human cells is not yet known.

Oil pressed from grape seeds is used as a dietary supplement. It contains a relatively high percentage of linoleic acid, which belongs to a group of nutrients known as essential fatty acids (EFAs). The body needs EFAs to regulate activities that include heart function, insulin utilisation, and mood balance. However, the body cannot produce EFAs, so they must be obtained from foods or dietary supplements. EFAs are thought to block the production of chemicals that promote the formation of deposits in the blood vessels. Consequently, blood pressure and blood cholesterol levels may be lowered and the risk of heart disease may decrease.

19) **Tulsi** (*Ocimum tenuiflorum*)

Ocimum tenuiflorum is an aromatic plant in the family Lamiaceae native throughout the Old World tropics and widespread as a cultivated plant and an escaped weed. It is cultivated for religious and medicinal purposes, and for its essential oil. There are two main morphotypes cultivated in India—green-leaved (Sri or Lakshmi Tulsi) and purple-leaved (Krishna Tulsi). It is known across South Asia as a medicinal plant, commonly used in Ayurveda, and has an important role within the Vaishnavite tradition of Hinduism, in which devotees perform worship involving Tulsi plants or leaves.

Tulsi flowers

Tulsi is an important symbol in many Hindu religious traditions which link the plant with the Goddess figure described in the Puranas. The name "Tulsi" in Sanskrit means "the incomparable one". The Tulsi plant is known in India in two forms—dark or Shyama (Krishna) Tulsi and light or Rama Tulsi. Rama Tulsi is commonly used for worship. Tulsi is regarded as a goddess (an avatar of Lakshmi) and a consort of Vishnu. A garland of Tulsi leaves is the first offering to the Lord as part of the daily ritual. Tulsi is accorded the sixth place among the eight objects of worship in the ritual of the consecration of the kalasha, the container of holy water.

According to one story, Tulsi was a gopi who fell in love with Krishna and so had a curse laid on her by His consort Radha. She is very dear to Vishnu. Tulsi is also mentioned in the stories of Mira and Radha immortalised in Jayadeva's Gita Govinda. One story has it that when Krishna was weighed in gold, not even all the ornaments of His consort Satyabhama could outweigh Him. But a single Tulsi leaf placed on one side by his consort Rukmini tilted the scale.

Tulsi is ceremonially married to Vishnu annually on the eleventh bright day of the month of Kaartika in the lunisolar calendar. This festival continues for five days and concludes on the full moon day, which falls in mid-October. This ritual, called the "Tulsi Vivaha", inaugurates the annual marriage season in India.

Medicinal uses and scientific research

Tulsi has been used for thousands of years in Ayurveda for its diverse healing properties. It is mentioned by Charaka in the Charaka Samhita, an ancient Ayurvedic text. Marked by its strong aroma and astringent taste, it is regarded in Ayurveda as a kind of "elixir of life" and believed to promote longevity.

Tulsi's extracts are used in ayurvedic remedies for common colds, headaches, stomach disorders, inflammation, heart disease, various forms of poisoning, and malaria. Traditionally, Tulsi is taken in many forms: as herbal tea, dried powder, fresh leaf, or mixed with ghee. Essential oil extracted from Karpoora Tulsi is mostly used for medicinal purposes and in herbal cosmetics, and is widely used in skin preparations due to its anti-bacterial activity. For centuries, the dried leaves of Tulsi have been mixed with stored grains to repel insects.

Recent studies suggest that Tulsi may be a COX-2 inhibitor, like many modern painkillers, due to its high concentration of eugenol (1-hydroxy-2-methoxy-4-allylbenzene). One study showed Tulsi to be an effective treatment for diabetes by reducing blood glucose levels. The same study showed significant reduction in total cholesterol levels with Tulsi. Another study showed that Tulsi's beneficial effect on blood glucose levels is due to its antioxidant properties. Tulsi also shows some promise for protection from radiation poisoning and cataracts.

In modern medicine, Holy Basil is considered an adaptogen, which means that it assists the body adapt to stress (environmental, physical, or chemical), restore balance in the body, and normalise body functions. It is currently being studied for its beneficial properties and has been found to be effective for cancer, diabetes, high cholesterol levels, stress, wound healing, the immune system, inflammations, liver support and protection, hypoglycemic conditions, ulcers, digestion, chronic fatigue syndrome, arthritis, radiation poisoning, cataracts, the memory, respiratory system, urinary problems, eczema, psoriasis and other skin conditions, and it is an antioxidant.

A study by the Delhi Institute of Pharmaceutical Sciences and Research from the University of Delhi in India overviewed the biological activities of Tulsi oil and concluded that:

- The oil possesses anti-inflammatory activity due to dual inhibition of arachidonate metabolism supplemented by antihistaminic activity. The anti-inflammatory activity is not dependent on the pituitary adrenal axis.

- The oil possesses antipyretic activity due to prostaglandin inhibition and peripherally acting analgesic activity.

- The oil has been found to be effective against formaldehyde or adjuvant induced arthritis and turpentine oil induced joint oedema in animals.

- Lipoxygenase inhibitory, histamine antagonistic and antisecretory activities of the oil contribute towards antiulcer activity.

- The oil can inhibit enhancement of vascular capillary permeability and leucocyte migration following inflammatory stimulus.

- The LD50 of the oil is 42.5 ml/kg and long-term use of oil at 3 ml/kg dose does not produce any untoward effects in rats.

- The oil contains a-linolenic acid, an omega-3 fatty acid, which on metabolism produces eicosapentaenoic acid and the same appears to be responsible for the biological activity.

- The oil has hypotensive, anticoagulant and immunomodulatory activities.

- Antioxidant property of the oil renders metabolic inhibition, chemoprevention and hypolipidaemic activity.

- Presence of linolenic acid in the oil imparts antibacterial activity against Staphylococcus aureus.

- The oil alone or in combination with cloxacillin, a beta-lactamase resistant penicillin, has been found to be beneficial in bovine mastitis, an inflammatory disorder resulting from staphylococcal infection.

- Existence of anti-inflammatory, analgesic and antibacterial activities in single entity i.e. fixed oil appears to be unique.

20) **Cinnamon** (*Cinnamomum verum*)

Cinnamon (Cinnamomum verum, synonym C. zeylanicum) is a small evergreen tree 10–15 metres (32.8–49.2 feet) tall, belonging to the family Lauraceae, and is native to Sri Lanka. The bark is widely used as a spice due to its distinct odour. Its flavour is due to an aromatic essential oil that makes up 0.5% to 1% of its composition. This oil is prepared by roughly pounding the bark, macerating it in seawater, and then quickly distilling the whole. It is of a golden-yellow colour, with the characteristic odour of cinnamon and a very hot aromatic taste. The pungent taste and scent come from cinnamic aldehyde or cinnamaldehyde and, by the absorption of oxygen as it ages, it darkens in colour and develops resinous compounds. Chemical components of the essential oil include ethyl cinnamate, eugenol, cinnamaldehyde, beta-caryophyllene, linalool, and methyl chavicol.

The name cinnamon comes from Greek kinnámōmon, itself ultimately from Phoenician. The botanical name for the spice - Cinnamomum zeylanicum - is derived from Sri Lanka's former (colonial) name, Ceylon.

Rolls of dried Cinnamon bark

History

Cinnamon has been known from remote antiquity, and it was so highly prized among ancient nations that it was regarded as a gift fit for monarchs and other great potentates. It was imported to Egypt from China as early as 2000 BC. It is mentioned in the Bible in Exodus 30:23, where Moses is commanded to use both sweet cinnamon and cassia in the holy anointing oil; in Proverbs 7:17–18, where the lover's bed is perfumed with myrrh, aloe and cinnamon; and in Song of

Solomon 4:14, a song describing the beauty of his beloved, cinnamon scents her garments like the smell of Lebanon. It is also alluded to by Herodotus and other classical writers and it was commonly used on funeral pyres in Rome. The Emperor Nero is said to have burned a year's supply of cinnamon at the funeral for his wife Poppaea Sabina in 65 AD.

Up to the Middle Ages, the source of cinnamon was a mystery to the Western world. It is possible that the Arabs established an early monopoly on trading in cinnamon, and kept its origin a secret for hundreds of years. In Herodotus and other authors, Arabia was the source of cinnamon: giant Cinnamon birds collected the cinnamon sticks from an unknown land where the cinnamon trees grew, and used them to construct their nests; the Arabs employed a trick to obtain the sticks. This story was current as late as 1310 in Byzantium, although in the first century, Pliny the Elder had written that the traders had made this up in order to charge more. The first mention of the spice growing in Sri Lanka was in Zakariya al-Qazwini's Athar al-bilad wa-akhbar al-'ibad ("Monument of Places and History of God's Bondsmen") in about 1270. This was followed shortly thereafter by John of Montecorvino, in a letter of about 1292.

Cinnamon has been cultivated from time immemorial in Sri Lanka, and the tree is also grown commercially at Tellicherry in southern India, Bangladesh, Java, Sumatra, the West Indies, Brazil, Vietnam, Madagascar, Zanzibar, and Egypt. Sri Lanka cinnamon has a very thin, smooth bark with a light-yellowish brown colour and a highly fragrant aroma.

Medicinal uses and scientific research

Cinnamon bark is widely used as a spice. It is principally employed in cookery as a condiment and flavouring material. It used in the preparation of chocolate, especially in Mexico, which is the main importer of true cinnamon. It is also used in the preparation of some kinds of desserts, such as apple pie and cinnamon buns as well as spicy candies, tea, hot cocoa, and liqueurs. Cinnamon bark is one of the few spices that can be consumed directly.

In medicine it acts like other volatile oils and once had a reputation as a cure for colds. It has also been used to treat diarrhoea and other problems of the digestive system. Cinnamon is high in antioxidant activity and the essential oil of cinnamon also has antimicrobial properties, which can aid in the preservation of certain foods.

The German Commission E recommended cinnamon for treating loss of appetite and stomach upset, and cinnamon teas have been used for centuries to prevent bloating and flatulence and to treat heartburn and nausea. Cinnamon's beneficial effects on the digestive tract are attributed to its antioxidant catechins, chemical compounds that are also found in tea.

Cinnamon antioxidants may also fight bacterial, fungal, and parasitic infections, especially yeast infections of the mouth (oral candidiasis) in people with compromised immune systems. There are some scientific indications that cinnamon relieves the pain of ulcers, and the herb is also very useful in regulating the activity of insulin, so effective, in fact, that diabetics may need to check their sugars more often if they eat large quantities (more than 1 tablespoon) of cinnamon every day. Cinnamon does not stimulate the release of insulin, but it helps insulin work more effectively. Recent advancement in phytochemistry has shown that it is a cinnamtannin B1 isolated from C. zeylanicum, which is of therapeutic effect on type II diabetes. Cinnamon has traditionally been used to treat toothache and fight bad breath and its regular use is believed to stave off common cold and aid digestion.

Cinnamon has been proposed for use as an insect repellent, although it remains untested and cinnamon leaf oil has been found to be very effective in killing mosquito larvae. The compounds cinnamaldehyde, cinnamyl acetate, eugenol and anethole, that are contained in cinnamon leaf oil, were found to have the highest effectiveness against mosquito larvae. It is reported that regularly drinking of Cinnamomum zeylanicum tea made from the bark could be beneficial to oxidative stress related illness in humans, as the plant part contains significant antioxidant potential.

A study by the Arizona Cancer Center, University of Arizona demonstrates that the cinnamon-derived dietary Michael acceptor trans-cinnamic aldehyde (CA) impairs melanoma cell proliferation and tumour growth. These findings support a previously unrecognised role of CA as a dietary Michael acceptor with potential anti-cancer activity.

21) **Rhododendron caucasicum**

In the Republic of Georgia, formerly part of the Soviet Union, it is not unusual for people to live beyond 100 years of age as active members of society. It has been theorised that their long lives may be attributed to regular consumption of a traditional yogurt called Kefir and flavonoid-rich foods such as wine and honey, along with a special tea that contains Rhododendron caucasicum.

The last verifiable statistics from the Republic of Georgia show that there are almost 23,000 Georgians over the age of 100 based on a population of only 3.2 million people. Grown at 10,000 to 30,000 foot elevations in the Caucasian Mountains, Rhododendron caucasicum (also known as "snow rose") contains polyphenolics, including flavonoids and proanthocyanidins.

R.caucasicum in flower

A Russian scientific research project dedicated to understanding the longevity of Georgian people discovered that they traditionally brewed the roots of their Snow Rose into what they called Alpine Tea and added it to their widely used Kefir culture, which proved to be the key to their longevity. The reasons they did so were three-fold. The Alpine Tea or Rhododendron caucasicum sweetened the Kefir culture, while protecting it from harmful bacteria, or from turning rancid before it could be eaten. They learned over a long period of time that this tea gave them strength and energy. They also discovered that it protected them from what today we call "free radicals, pathogens, and viruses", but to them it just seemed to ward off many diseases from which their neighbours in surrounding countries were always dying of.

The scientists learned that the Rhododendron caucasicum has many important properties of its own. It improves physical abilities, increases activity of the cardiovascular system, and increases blood supply to muscles and especially to the brain. It also shows tremendous anti-bacterial activity against the harmful bacteria, but allows "friendly" or probiotics, such as are found in Kefir culture, to thrive.

Rhododendron caucasicum is a unique plant among all other species of Rhododendron and is considered safe for human consumption. It is reported that some Rhododendrons, mainly the flowers, contain grayanotoxins, which are not soluble in water and can be harmful. Therefore, do not just go out to your garden and harvest your backyard Rhododendron!

Medicinal uses and scientific research

Professor Dr. Zakir Ramazanov, Ph.D. explains that thirty years of research indicate that the phenylpropanoids in Rhododendron improve physical abilities, increase activity of the cardiovascular system, and increase blood supply to the muscles and especially to the brain. Rhododendron caucasicum increases resistance of the brain to imbalances due to chemical, physical, and biological reasons. It also is an antibacterial while allowing the good probiotics to thrive. It acts as a detoxicant, is highly P-vitamin active, protecting against capillary fragility, and is an excellent free-radical scavenger. Studies have demonstrated that Rhododendron caucasicum inhibits or abolishes the activity of the enzyme hyaluronidase, known to be an initiator of colon cancer.

Clinical research has been ongoing as to the medicinal uses of this alpine plant. Prof. Dimitry M. Rossiyski, M.D., Meritorious Science Worker at the Soviet Medical Academy of Science, conducted a double-blind placebo study on seventy test subjects diagnosed with circulatory insufficiency and atherosclerosis, some with high blood pressure and evidence of past heart attacks. A 30 mg/day dose of Rhododendron extract over a 15-day period resulted in the subjects experiencing a lowered blood pressure, improvement in coronary circulation, decrease of serum cholesterol, and elimination of pain in the chest area.

Subsequent studies at the First Central Moscow Hospital showed similar results on heart patients suffering from hardening of the arteries. Doctors Avraamova and

Galperin performed clinical studies at the Moscow State Hospital on 24 males and 36 females ages 18-65 diagnosed with mitral valve insufficiency (prolapse). Improvements were obvious in the patients taking Rhododendron extract over those who did not receive it. The average hearts in those receiving the extract were lowered from 90 to 70 beats per minute and systolic blood pressure was lowered from 177 to 160 mm Hg (Rossiysky 1954).

Again, studies at the First Central Moscow Hospital revealed that when 50 mg of Rhododendron caucasicum diluted in water was given to 170 volunteers suffering from severe gout, the average discharge of uric acid increased 55-60 percent and pain was relieved in a few hours. The Georgian Academy of Sciences gave 50 to 100 mg per day of the snow rose to 114 patients hospitalized for depression. The results showed a marked decrease in depressive symptoms in 93 of the patients. Similar results were achieved by the Moscow State Hospital study, indicating improvement of 162 patients with severe depression.

One of the key benefits for anti-aging is Rhododendron caucasicum's inhibition of hyaluronidase activity and its subsequent benefit to osteoarthritis patients. One theory regarding the cause of arthritis is that it may appear because of the abnormal release of the enzyme hyaluronidase from the cartilage cells. This leads to cartilage breakdown and destruction of the joint. Perhaps its inhibition of hyaluronidase activity is the key to arthritis prevention.

R. caucasicum is also highly antibacterial, perhaps due to the presence of the well-known antibacterial compounds chlorogenic and caffeic acids that are known to exist in this plant. Tests conclude that it is more effective than either grape seed or pine bark as an antibacterial proanthocyanidin. In a 24-hour test of 12,000 Staphylococcus aureus bacteria thriving in solution, all were totally eliminated by Rhododendron, but 300 colonies were still surviving in the grape seed petri dish, and 370 in the pine bark solution.

22) **Bamboo leaf** *(Lophatherum gracile)*

Bamboo is best known for its hard stems (culms) that are used in place of wood for a variety of applications, including furniture, scaffolding, flutes, fence posts, flooring, and even bicycle frames. Bamboos also serve as decorative plants, the source of tender shoots used in Chinese cuisine, and a primary subject of many Chinese artworks. Early Chinese books were written on bamboo slats and bamboo has been used as a source of medicine since ancient times.

The leaves most frequently used in Chinese herbal medicine are collected from another plant, Lophatherum gracile, the grass bamboo, one of the smallest of the bamboo-like plants. The leaves and stem of a small bamboo-like plant, Lophatherum gracile, are collected and dried and in Japan, the leaves of the black bamboo are used similarly.

Bamboo leaves

Medicinal use and scientific research

Bamboo leaf has a long history of food and medical application in China and has recently been listed by Ministry of Health PRC into the list of natural plants with dual-purposes as food and drug.

In traditional Chinese medicine, bamboo leaves are believed to be beneficial for the mind, as it produces a positive effect on the heart. They are used to heal and treat fever, fidgeting, urinary retention with blood in the urine and lung inflammation. Bamboo leaf and bamboo shavings are both commonly used in cases of stomach heat, providing a cooling effect and helping counter the perverse flow of "qi" (upward flow instead of the normal downward flow).

Effective ingredients of bamboo leaf extract include flavone, phenolic acid, lactone, polyose, amino acids active peptide, manganese, zinc, and selenium with enhanced effects against anti-free radical and blood vessel disease. It is also effective in liver protection, expansion of blood capillaries, smoothing microcirculation, improving retentive faculty and improving sleep quality. The bamboo leaf flavones are a key ingredient within the function of blood-lipid regulation. Clinical experiments show that it is a safe and effective health food that applies to different kinds of blood-lipid abnormalities. It is also effective in anti-oxidation, anti-fatigue, immunity-enhancement, anti-inflammation, sleep improvement, and beautification.

Bamboo leaf has raised the attention of state authorities and international and domestic scientific circles due to its well recognised positive impacts on the health and longevity of human beings. Japanese scientists have discovered that the internal structure of bamboo leaf flavonoid is similar to that of hemoglobin of human beings.

It is generally known that bamboo leaf flavoniod is very safe without any toxicity. Bamboo leaf extract also presents also very good technical features as it is easy to dissolve in hot water and low-density alcohol with high thermal and water stability, processing flexibility and high oxidation prevention stability. Even under unfavorable conditions, the local concentration far exceeds the norms and there are no oxidation promotion effects, which generally occur in tea polyphenols.

Research done at Shanghai First People's Hospital has showed that the flavone from bamboo leaf can eliminate various active oxygen-derived free radicals, inhibit the peroxidation of lipids, cleanse blood vessels, and has good effect on cardio-cerebral vascular protection. Furthermore, flavone extracted from bamboo leaf also has a good immunoregulation function that will significantly promote the resistance of body to adverse environment and diseases. Compared with normal flavones, bamboo leaf flavone has advantages in its stable structure, resistance to degradation, and direct effect on deep lesion access.

23) Grape seed extract (*Vitis Vinifera*)

Grape seed extracts are industrial derivatives from whole grape seeds. Typically, the commercial opportunity of extracting grape seed constituents has been for chemicals known as polyphenols, including oligomeric proanthocyanidins recognized as antioxidants.

Medicinal use and scientific research

Human case reports and results from laboratory and animal studies show that grape seed extract may be useful to treat heart diseases such as high blood pressure and high cholesterol. By limiting lipid oxidation, phenolics in grape seeds may reduce risk of heart disease, such as by inhibiting platelet aggregation and reducing inflammation.

A polyphenol contained in grape seeds is resveratrol which may interfere with cancer cell growth and proliferation, as well as induce apoptosis, among a variety of potential chemopreventive effects.

Grape seed components may also be active against HIV by inhibiting virus expression and replication.

Preliminary research shows that grape seed extract may have other possible anti-disease properties, such as in laboratory models of

* wound healing—grape seed proanthocyanidins induced vascular endothelial growth factor and accelerated healing of injured skin in mice.
* tooth decay --seed phenolics may inhibit oral sugar metabolism and retard growth of certain bacteria causing dental caries.
* osteoporosis -- grape seed extracts enhanced bone density and strength in experimental animals.
* skin cancer -- grape seed proanthocyanidins decreased tumour numbers and reduced the malignancy of papillomas.
* ultraviolet damage to skin—dietary proanthocyanidins may protect against carcinogenesis and provide supplementation for sunscreen protection.

A new study conducted at the University of Kentucky in the United States, and published in the journal Clinical Cancer Research, found that leukaemia cancer cells exposed to grape seed extract (GSE) were rapidly killed through a process of cell suicide known as "apoptosis."

In these laboratory studies, an astonishing 76% of leukaemia cells committed suicide within 24 hours thanks to the ability of GSE to activate a protein called JNK, which regulates apoptosis. When the mechanism behind apoptosis breaks down, cancerous cells can survive and multiply. When they exposed the leukaemia cells to an agent that inhibits JNK, the grape seed extract effect was cancelled out. Silencing the gene that makes JNK also blocked the extract's ability to kill cancer cells.

In a healthy person, cancer cell apoptosis is a normal, healthy part of biology. Every living system creates cancerous cells. There are hundreds or thousands of "microtumours" in every human being living today, but cancerous cells in healthy people destroy themselves once they realise they're flawed. This cellular "realisation," however, requires healthy cell communication, and that's dependent on the correct nutrients, minerals and proteins being available in the body.

Grape seed extract appears to accelerate this process in cancer cells, helping them more rapidly assess their own flawed state so they can engage in apoptosis (cell suicide), thus protecting the larger organism (the body).

It's important to note that this recent study was conducted in a lab, not in human beings, so its conclusions cannot necessarily be directly translated into saying something like "grape seed extract cures cancer," for example. However, it does indicate quite convincingly that if the unique phytochemical molecules found in grape seed extract can be delivered to leukaemia cells with sufficient potency, they may play an important role in cancer cells destroying themselves, thereby protecting the whole organism from runaway cancer.

If the results demonstrated in the labs at the University of Kentucky can be replicated in humans, it could potentially position grape seed extract as one of the most powerful natural chemotherapeutic agents yet discovered. Previous research has shown grape seed extract has an effect on skin, breast, bowel, lung, stomach and prostate cancer cells in the laboratory. It can also reduce the size of breast tumours in rats and skin tumours in mice. However, the University of Kentucky study is the first to test its impact on a blood cancer.

Lead researcher Professor Xianglin Shi said: "These results could have implications for the incorporation of agents such as grape seed extract into prevention or treatment of haematological (blood) malignancies and possibly other cancers. "What everyone seeks is an agent that has an effect on cancer cells but leaves normal cells alone, and this shows that grape seed extract fits into this category." This is a natural method of getting rid of damaged and potentially dangerous cells.

Grape seed extract has been studied and demonstrated to be remarkably effective at killing cancer cells for many different types of cancer, by the way, including cancers of the breast, prostate, lung, skin bowel and stomach.

A study of 40 people with high cholesterol assessed the effects of grape seed extract, chromium, a combination of both, or placebo for 2 months. The combination of grape seed extract and chromium was more effective than either substance alone or placebo in reducing total and LDL ("bad") cholesterol.

A more recent study tested the effects of a patented grape seed extract on lipid peroxidation (which aids in the formation of "bad" cholesterol) in a group of heavy smokers. Twenty-four healthy male smokers, (aged 50 years or greater) were given either placebo or 2 capsules (75 mg of a grape procyanidin extracts and soy-phosphatidalcholine), twice daily for 4 weeks. "Bad" cholesterol levels (low density lipoprotein or LDL) were lower in those taking the grape seed supplement than those on placebo. The authors concluded that grape seed extract may help prevent cholesterol oxidation and further damage to the cardiovascular system in people who smoke.

Antioxidants, such as grape seed, help protect blood vessels from damage. Damaged blood vessels can lead to an increased demand on the heart. In several animal studies, a grape seed extract substantially reduced blood pressure. Human studies are needed to determine whether grape seed extract confers the same benefits to people with high blood pressure.

In one recent study of only three patients with chronic pancreatitis (inflammation of the pancreas), a commercially available grape seed extract significantly reduced the frequency and intensity of abdominal pain after conventional medications failed to improve symptoms.

24) Himalayan Pink Salt

Himalayan Pink Salt is a term for rock salt from Pakistan, which began being sold by various companies in Europe, North America, and Australia in the early 21st century. It is mined in the Khewra Salt Mines, the second largest salt mine in the world, located in Khewra, Jhelum District, Punjab, Pakistan, about 160 kilometres from Islamabad and 260 kilometres from Lahore, and in the foothills of the Salt Range.

The salt sometimes comes out in a reddish or pink colour, with some crystals having an off-white to transparent colour. Himalayan salt is also used the same way as regular salt, as food seasoning and in some drinks. Himalayan salt is also used as Kosher salt due to having a much larger grain size. It has a subtle difference in taste from regular table salt that some say makes it taste better. It is also commonly used for brine, and bath products.

Himalayan salt rocks

History

Himalayan Pink Salt originally formed from marine fossil deposits over 250 million years ago during the Jurassic era. Harvested from ancient sea beds in the Himalayan foothills, this rare and extraordinary salt has been a valuable commodity for centuries. Historically, the Himalayan people used this salt to preserve their fish and meat throughout the year, and every spring they transported the salt to Nepalese valleys for trade. Heavily burdened yaks would carry the salt along narrow sloping paths, mountains, and cliffs in order to sell and exchange the salt for other commodities.

Himalayan Pink Salt is still extracted from mines by hand, according to long-standing tradition, and without the use of any mechanical devices or explosion techniques. After being hand-selected, the salt is then hand-crushed, hand-washed, and dried in the sun.

More recently, large crystal rocks are also used as lamps. These large crystal rocks are carved into their desired shape and size. The final shape of the crystal rock are then mounted on a wooden base for stability and an electrical bulb is fixed within the crystals' hollow area to illuminate the whole rock when it is lit. This is said to harmonise the energy of the space the lamp is lit in.

Himalayan salt plates are used in presentation and culinary settings. Salt plates can be carefully heated and used to sear food such as vegetables, fish, shrimp or thin slices of steak. The food is cooked and seasoned simultaneously. Salt plates can also be used as a serving tray for sushi, vegetables, cheese, or other bite-sized foods.

Mineral composition

The Bavarian consumer protection agency Bayerisches Landesamt für Gesundheit und Lebensmittelsicherheit analyzed in 2003 15 specimens of Himalaya salt sold in Germany and could detect a total of 10 different minerals: sodium and chloride (98%) and other trace minerals such as magnesium 0.07%, sulfate 0.05% and iron 0.0006%. German public television broadcaster ZDF presented the analyzed chemical composition of Himalaya-salt made by mineralogist Michael Siemann of the technical university of Clausthal (TU Clausthal Germany) who states that the specimen contained 95-96% sodium chloride and 10 different minerals, the same as the above.

Medicinal uses

Himalayan Pink Salt in the form of brine is used in tooth brushing for gum bleeding and is also used to remedy certain skin conditions such as foot fungus. The brine is also is used for a plethora of physical ailments including arthritis, rheumatism, osteoporosis, gout, kidney and gall bladder stones, skin diseases, psoriasis, and for toxin elimination.

Externally, a brine bath is recommended for detoxification, to strengthen the immune system, heal skin diseases, for rheumatism and joint diseases, to balance the skin's pH, and for recovery after surgery. Himalayan salt is used as an ingredient in making bath additives such as bath salts, bath bombs, and other related products like scrubs.

Himalayan Pink Salt provides essential minerals, trace elements, balances electrolytes, supports proper nutrient absorption, eliminates toxins, balances the body's pH, normalises blood pressure, and increases circulation and conductivity. It can also assist with relief from arthritis, skin rashes, psoriasis, herpes, and flu and fever symptoms.

Externally, pink salt can be used to stimulate circulation, relax the body, lower blood pressure, soothe sore muscles, and remove toxins from the body.

25) **Monatomic rhodium**

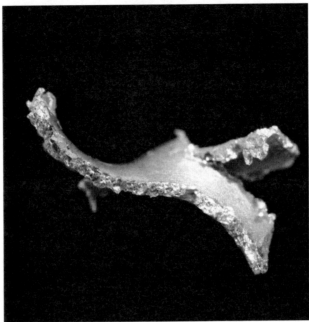

Rhodium in its solid metallic form

Monatomic rhodium (also spelled monoatomic) has been used on this planet since the dawn of time to greatly accelerate the evolution of consciousness. Egyptian as well as other sacred civilisations and spiritual schools have utilised this little-known spiritual biochemistry. It is unique in form and function and it has been theorised that the elongated nuclei of monatomic elements allow for a high spin state, along with "paired" electrons, making them biosuperconductors.

Monatomic rhodium facilitates a flow of energy through the body with little or no resistance: and that light continues to flow, even without additional external effort. Monatomic rhodium can transform blockages caused by the old programs that surface during inner growth by allowing a continual flow of light that ultimately washes away and heals, all the way down to the sub-atomic level. Monatomic Rhodium allows for the path of growth through struggle to fall away, opening you to a more joyous process.

History

Since ancient Egyptian times, alchemists have discreetly worked to produce something called the Philosopher's Stone, or the Elixir of Life. David Hudson and other researchers have found materials that are believed to be related to the

Philosopher's Stone. The materials have been called ORMEs, monatomic gold, white gold, white powder gold, ORMUS, m-state, AuM, microclusters, and manna. David Hudson calls the materials he found Orbitally Rearranged Monatomic Elements or ORMEs. He also refers to them as monatomic elements in a high-spin state.

The Chemistry and Physics of Monatomic Elements, describes the characteristics of those elements which have come to be known as the "Precious Metals". These eight metals include: ruthenium, rhodium, palladium, and silver (known as the "light platinum group"), osmium, iridium, platinum, and gold (known as the "heavy platinum group"). These elements can in a monatomic, superdeformed, high spin, and low energy state, lose their chemical reactivity and metallic nature -- thereby resulting in a state of Superconductivity -- a resonant condition complete with Meissner magnetic fields, Cooper Pairs, and electrons which have literally changed into light (i.e. photons).

These precious metals have the unique ability to remain stable in the monatomic form, which can then lead to very powerful effects in fundamental biological and human physiological effects.

Of particular importance is the fact that all of these precious metals have a strong affinity for and are almost always found in their natural state in combination with gold. Gold, in turn, has a history of being the most precious of all commodities -- a "spiritual tradition" which has survived countless generations.

Alchemy books talk about "the White Powder of Gold", the Food of the Gods -- a substance derived from yellow gold, but which has been transformed into a white powder upon reaching its monatomic state. This is the same form, and may be equivalent to the same process by which scientist David Hudson found all eight of the monatomic precious metals.

For the alchemists, "The Master Work" was to prepare the Elixir of Life and The Philosopher's Stone -- or in more anecdotal, traditional terms, transmute lead into gold.

In the quest to accomplish this noble work, the alchemists of old taught that the key to success was to "divide, divide, divide..." The implication of this advice is that only in freeing the atoms of an element from the confines of its crystalline-like metallic structure of many atoms of the same or diverse elements, could one hope to achieve the alchemists' esoteric goal. In effect, the alchemists were apparently attempting to reach the monatomic form of the gold and the other precious elements -- even if they might not have described the process as such.

Hudson has also connected the ORME with the Hebrew tradition of the Ma-Na or Manna -- also thought to be the White Powder of Gold. Curiously, manna means literally: "What is it?" This phrase is found repeated over and over again in The Egyptian Book of the Dead and The Papyrus of Ani. The historical and philosophical implications thus include the ORME as part of the metallurgical foundry at Qumran, where the Essenes are believed to have been located.

Other references include the mixture of the white powder of gold in water as being "that which issues from the mouth of the creator", "the semen of the father in heaven", and The Golden Tear from the Eye of Horus. Later in the Essene tradition, the white powder of gold began being referred to as the "teacher of righteousness", something which was swallowed and taken internally.

This latter point emphasises the point of approaching spiritual practices, including eating, with a profound sense of being in the presence of the divine.

The alchemists Lapidus and Eirenaeus Philalethes have said: "The Philosopher's Stone is no stone, but a powder with the power to transmute base metals into gold and silver." They go on to claim: "The stone which is to be the transformer of metals into gold must be sought in the precious metals in which it is enclosed and contained. It is called a stone by virtue of its fixed nature, and it resists the action of fire as successfully as any stone -- but its appearance is that of a very fine powder, impalpable to the touch, fragment as to smell, in potency a most penetrative spirit, apparently dry, and yet unctuous, and easily capable of tingeing a plate of metal. The stone does not exist in nature, but has to be prepared by art, in obedience to nature's laws. Thus, you see our stone is made of gold alone, yet it is not common gold."

Medicinal use and scientific research

The May 1995 issue of Scientific American discussed the effects of ruthenium (one of the precious metals), by noting that a single ruthenium atom placed at each end of the double-helix DNA increases the conductivity of the strand by a factor of 10,000, causing the DNA to become, in effect, a "superconductor". Hudson has noted in the Scientific Literature (Guidice, et al), the basis for human cells being able to exhibit Superconductivity and the extensive amount of research being conducted on treating cancer and other diseases with precious metals. These precious elements appear to be correcting the DNA, literally "flowing the light of life" within the body.

The Platinum Metals Review includes articles which discuss the treatment of cancers using platinum, iridium, and ruthenium. Apparently, the application of a platinum compound to an altered DNA state (as in the case of a cancer) will cause the DNA to relax and become corrected. It is known that both iridium and rhodium have anti-ageing properties, that ruthenium and platinum compounds interact with DNA, and that gold and the precious metals can activate the endocrinal glandular system in a way that heightens awareness and aptitude to extraordinary levels.

The ancients from thousands of years ago knew of the superconducting effect of the precious metals on our consciousness -- what they referred to as the light body (the ka), and that both the physical body and the light body had to be fed. In so doing, we can possibly use the properties of the monatomic elements to activate the body's so-called "junk DNA", along with the generally unused 90 to 95 % of the brain.

The good news is that the precious elements occur in herbs and numerous vegetables. Grapes, for example, can be a primary source. A four ounce glass of Concord grape juice frozen concentrate can yield 127 mg of rhodium and 48 mg of iridium (more than an equivalent amount of virtually any other food). A key to the grape's concentration of these precious metals is apparently connected to the fact that the grape roots go so much deeper into the Earth, where there is, apparently, a much better source of the elements. This explains why the deepest mines on Earth are gold mines, and furthermore that volcanoes are also a source. This implies that the interior of the Earth seems to be a primary "manufacturer" of the elements, and thus the ash from a volcanic eruption leaves downwind crop fields enormously fertile for years.

Monatomic rhodium and other ORME's have had many anecdotes reporting the activation of latent esoteric abilities in humans.

VI. GLOSSARY OF COMPOUNDS

Anti-Oxidants · Antioxidants are widely used as ingredients in dietary supplements in the hope of maintaining health and preventing diseases such as cancer and coronary heart disease. The use of antioxidants in pharmacology is intensively studied, particularly as treatments for stroke and neurodegenerative diseases. However, it is unknown whether oxidative stress is the cause or the consequence of disease.

An antioxidant is a molecule capable of slowing or preventing the oxidation of other molecules. Oxidation is a chemical reaction that transfers electrons from a substance to an oxidising agent. Oxidation reactions can produce free radicals, which start chain reactions that damage cells. Antioxidants terminate these chain reactions by removing free radical intermediates and inhibit other oxidation reactions by being oxidised themselves. As a result, antioxidants are often reducing agents such as thiols, ascorbic acid or polyphenols.

Alkaline · An alkali is a substance that has a high pH when in solution and tends to neutralise acids. The amount of alkali available in the body to act as a buffer, moderating changes in pH, is called the alkali reserve or standard bicarbonate (because most of the alkali is in the form of bicarbonate ions). Alkaline or acid produced by the body must have an equal and opposite acid or alkaline produced by the body.

Adaptogen · The term adaptogen is used by herbalists to refer to a natural herb product that is proposed to increase the body's resistance to stress, trauma, anxiety and fatigue. In the past, they have been called rejuvenating herbs, qi tonics, rasayanas, or restoratives. Adaptogen is an agent that allows the body to counter adverse physical, chemical, or biological stressors by raising nonspecific resistance toward such stress, thus allowing the organism to "adapt" to the stressful circumstances. Adaptogenic ingredients found in Theriaca Elixir are Jiaogulan, Suma, Maitake, Reishi, Liquorice and Tulsi.

Saponins · Saponins are a class of chemical compounds, one of many secondary metabolites found in natural sources, with saponins found in particular abundance in various plant species such as Jiaogulan and Suma. A ready and therapeutically relevant example is the cardio-active agent digoxin, from common foxglove. Studies have illustrated the beneficial effects on blood cholesterol levels, cancer, bone health and stimulation of the immune system.

Germanium · Germanium is a chemical element with the symbol Ge and atomic number 32. It is a lustrous, hard, greyish-white metalloid in the carbon group. A high intake of germanium is supposed to improve the immune system, boost the body's oxygen supply, make a person feel more alive and destroy damaging free radicals. In addition, it is said to protect the user against radiation. Germanium has been detected in the atmosphere of Jupiter and in some of the most distant stars but can be found much closer to us in the Suma ingredient of Theriaca Elixir.

Resveratrol · Resveratrol is a phytoalexin naturally produced by several plants when under attack by pathogens such as bacteria or fungi. Resveratrol has also been produced by chemical synthesis and is sold as a nutritional supplement derived primarily from Japanese knotweed. It is found in Theriaca Elixir in Muscadine and in Grape Seed Extract. Anti-cancer, anti-inflammatory, blood-sugar-lowering and other beneficial cardiovascular effects of resveratrol have been reported.

Beta-Glucans · Beta-glucans are polysaccharides of D-glucose monomers linked by glycosidic bonds. Beta-glucans are a diverse group of molecules which can vary with respect to molecular mass, solubility, viscosity, and three-dimensional configuration. They occur most commonly as cellulose in plants, the bran of cereal grains, the cell walls of baker's yeast, certain bacteria, fungi and mushrooms such as Coriolus Versicolor and Agaricus Blazei Murill. Some forms of beta-glucans are useful in human nutrition as texturing agents and as soluble fibre supplements. Yeast and medicinal mushroom derived beta-glucans are notable for their ability to modulate the immune system.

Trace Minerals · In biochemistry, a trace element is a chemical element that is needed in minute quantities for the proper growth, development, and physiology of the organism. A trace element is also referred to as a micronutrient. Minerals are inorganic elements that originate in the earth and cannot be made in the body. They play important roles in various bodily functions and are necessary to sustain life and maintain optimal health, and are thus essential nutrients. Most of the minerals in the human diet come directly from plants and water. A mineral is a naturally occurring solid formed through geological processes that has a characteristic chemical composition, a highly ordered atomic structure, and specific physical properties. The main sources of trace minerals in Theriaca Elixir are Himalayan Pink Salt and the alchemical Monatomic Rhodium.

Amino Acids · Amino acids are critical to life, and their most important function is their variety of roles in metabolism. One particularly important function is as the building blocks of proteins, which are linear chains of amino acids. Every protein is chemically defined by this primary structure, its unique sequence of amino acid residues, which in turn define the three-dimensional structure of the protein. Amino acids are also important in many other biological molecules, such as forming parts of coenzymes. Amino acids are very important in nutrition.

Enzymes · Enzymes are proteins that catalyse (i.e., increase the rates of) chemical reactions. In enzymatic reactions, the molecules at the beginning of the process are called substrates and the enzyme converts them into different molecules, called the products. Like all catalysts, enzymes work by lowering the activation energy. As with all catalysts, enzymes are not consumed by the reactions they catalyse, nor do they alter the equilibrium of these reactions. The importance of enzymes is shown by the fact that a lethal illness can be caused by the malfunction of just one type of enzyme out of the thousands of types present in our bodies.

The main known function of enzymes is to break down proteins into amino acids as well as breaking down complex sugars for digestion but they are being vastly researched for many potential healing properties.

Proteins · Proteins are organic compounds made of amino acids arranged in a linear chain and folded into a globular form. The sequence of amino acids in a protein is defined by the sequence of a gene, which is encoded in the genetic code. Proteins are essential parts of organisms and participate in virtually every process within cells. Many proteins are enzymes that catalyse biochemical reactions and are vital to metabolism. Proteins are also necessary in animals' diets, since animals cannot synthesise all the amino acids they need and must obtain essential amino acids from food. Through the process of digestion, animals break down ingested protein into free amino acids that are then used in metabolism.

Vitamins · A vitamin is an organic compound required as a nutrient in tiny amounts by an organism. A compound is called a vitamin when it cannot be synthesised in sufficient quantities by an organism, and must be obtained from the diet such as in Stinging Nettle, Sea Buckthorn or Shiitake in Theriaca Elixir. Vitamins have diverse biochemical functions, including function as hormones (e.g. vitamin D), antioxidants (e.g. vitamin E), mediators of cell signalling and regulators of cell and tissue growth and differentiation (e.g. vitamin A). The largest number of vitamins (e.g. B complex vitamins) function as precursors for enzyme cofactor bio-molecules (coenzymes), that help act as catalysts and substrates in metabolism.

Carbohydrates · A carbohydrate is an organic compound consisting only of carbon, hydrogen and oxygen, the last two in the 2:1 atom ratio. Carbohydrates can be viewed as hydrates of carbon, hence their name. It is essentially a synonym of saccharide, a large family of natural carbohydrates that fill numerous roles in living things, such as the storage and transport of energy (e.g., starch, glycogen) and structural components (e.g., cellulose in plants and chitin in arthropods). In food science and in many informal contexts, the term carbohydrate often means any food that is particularly rich in starch (such as cereals, bread and pasta) or sugar (such as candy, jams and desserts).

OPCs · Oligomeric proanthocyanidins or OPCs are a class of flavonoid complexes found in sea buckthorn oil and grape seeds and skin, that act as antioxidants (free radical scavengers) in the human body. OPCs may help protect against the effects of internal and environmental stresses such as cigarette smoking and pollution, as well as supporting normal body metabolic processes. The effects may include depressing blood fat, emolliating blood vessels, lowering blood pressure, preventing blood vessel scleroses, dropping blood viscidity and preventing thrombus formation.

Quercetin · Quercetin is a plant-derived flavonoid, specifically a flavonol, used as a nutritional supplement and in Theriaca Elixir, it is a component of the Pau d'Arco ingredient. The American Cancer Society says that quercetin "has been promoted as being effective against a wide variety of diseases, including cancer," and "some early lab results appear promising". Quercetin has demonstrated significant anti-inflammatory activity by inhibiting both manufacture and release of histamine and other allergic/inflammatory mediators. In addition, it exerts potent antioxidant activity and vitamin C-sparing action.

VII. SPIRITUALITY AND FINANCIAL ABUNDANCE

Theriaca Elixir was created as a service to humanity. After drinking this wonderful brew your experience of this amazingly healing and powerfully rejuvenating tea will naturally create the feeling of wanting to share this product with everyone you know...your community, your family, your friends and the many friends that you will make who will discover also how to empower body, mind and spirit.

This will not simply be a business but rather a path, an opportunity that you can share and in doing so prosper on all levels.

Theriaca Elixir is also an opportunity for financial as well as physical well-being. Theriaca Elixir's core mission is to empower the world by bringing health and vitality to thousands of people worldwide and by providing this nutritional and psychological support, embracing the power within each of us to make a real difference in people's lives.

As Tony Samara explains, "A healthy mind, healthy body and healthy emotions create a natural flow of energy that is prosperity in the true sense."

Many of us feel that spirituality is renouncing the joys, the abundance, the freedom of being alive in a complete sense but by embracing an abundant, balanced life, good health and longevity (not just in relation to the body) we can create a complete philosophy that encompasses body, mind and emotions.

Financial abundance like spirituality is primarily about sharing and trusting, going beyond our personal limitations and fears, embracing and dealing with who we are in a practical and real sense - energetically as well as financially. If we are connected to an energy field that encompasses financial anxiety and limited belief systems then we connect our anxieties and limitations to all that we do, including negating our financial well-being.

This is a very common experience, more common than you think and is very unpleasant and totally unnecessary as a healthy means of expressing our wonderful being. These limiting beliefs can only be useful if dealt with in a way that helps us to grow beyond these limitations.

This experience is not only personal but also encompasses our human history as it stems back to our cultural and genetic experiences. By observing history over thousands of years we can see that humanity's mass fear, focussed around survival, has impacted negatively around money. By focussing on the thought of having no or not enough money brings up real consequences that our ancestors and many people today struggle with.

In the most severe cases we can become prone to great lacks, corruption, shame, failure, worthlessness and a sense of meaninglessness and are unable to partake in the abundance of life. So often we fill our energies with the fear of such consequences by bringing our thoughts and level of awareness to basic survival mode. Instead of freely sharing a sense of joyous celebration and living with a sense of gratitude for the many possibilities we are blind to the possibilities by the sense of lack and its many expressions.

When we personally experience and live with such anxiety we connect ourselves to the law of natural resonance whereby whatever we put out energetically, mentally, physically and emotionally attracts to itself experiences that resonate with itself rather than experiences that move us beyond such suffering.

When our experiences resonate with such personal limitations then we also attract the historical and present human collective anxiety around this issue. Rich or poor this experience of there not being enough is very unpleasant. What is the solution?

An important part of the solution would be to realise that a lot of what we are investing in whether it be feelings, thoughts or even real experiences stem from destructive thinking and that it is this thinking that is attracting the feelings and realities of lack - lack of all that creates a feeling of aliveness and rather reinforces the reality of lack and not enough.

The first step would be to change such thinking by perhaps visualising or internally experiencing that this lack is simply a thought, an energy form, and can with practise be replaced with thoughts that better serve you, your family and your community.

This is perhaps done by relaxing, breathing and contemplating what it is like to be abundant in the things that create deep happiness for yourself and your community.

You can enjoy the dream of prosperity in this state, not simply in the mind but also in the body sensations and warm feelings that go with it. This creates confidence and a feeling of safety that the new thought that you are embracing can become your reality. As Tony Samara says, "Your inner world reflects the outside, as the outside reflects the inside."

It is not simply the outer object of money that creates this safety and happiness, as when you meet many rich people they will tell you they are suffering from the same sense of lack as people who have nothing. So by facing the spiritual sense of prosperity you can separate the material from the psychological and hence empower your thoughts to correspond with the material level, creating real abundant happiness and safety. You can also in the same way empower your thoughts to correspond to the emotional and mental levels of your being creating freedom from the sense of lack that blinds you from all the joy of being alive in a complete sense.

It is very important to be honest about these belief systems and thereby be realistic rather than using this exercise to compensate for a sense of lack. Use this exercise for spiritual prosperity and psychological contentment so that you are free flowing with the spirit of the universe rather than swimming against the stream of life.

As you are open to receiving that which naturally comes with this flow you learn to surrender and give yourself to true love and compassion. This is of course easily achieved when we feel of service to others and it creates a sense of wisdom and freedom that flows into abundance on the material level. Such abundance also requires managing the material level with dignity and generosity and understanding that love is eternal and has no limitations.

Thinking in this way is not just a simple meditation or a type of school work but rather an art like the graceful art of drinking tea in Japan. It is not simply the outcome or result that is important but rather the consciousness and act itself. If you act in a truly generous way then this thinking becomes your personal law over a period of time and with every such empowering thought you give more energy to thoughts that are similar in nature and thus reach a higher level within yourself and touch a perspective of understanding that is much more closely aligned to the natural abundance of life. As this art of thinking is repeated then the body and emotions begin to change to encompass this as your personal law and way of life.

The negative, fixed and rigid thoughts somehow disappear. Our unconscious thinking, which may say that I am poor, I am no good at this, I am too fat or too stupid or I will never achieve my goals changes and hence empowers an abundant form of consciousness rather than poverty consciousness.

VIII. THE JOURNEY OF A LIFETIME BEGINS WITH A FEW EASY STEPS

When we are no longer trapped in the negative thoughts then we can move on to open our unconscious thinking to the powerful hope and recognition of change. This doesn't mean escaping from the reality that we are living in but rather acknowledging our thoughts as real and hence an amazing step that prepares us to get ready to think differently.

Often we fill our energies with the fear of such consequences by bringing our thoughts and level of awareness to basic survival mode instead of freely sharing a sense of joyous celebration and living with a sense of gratitude for the many possibilities we are blind to the possibilities by the sense of lack and its many expressions.

These steps are perhaps best taken by relaxing, breathing and contemplating what it is like to be abundant in the things that create deep happiness for yourself and your community. You can enjoy the dream of prosperity in this state, not simply in the mind but also in the body sensations and warm feelings that go with it. This creates confidence and a feeling of safety that the new thought that you are embracing can become your reality. As Tony Samara says, "Your inner world reflects the outside, as the outside reflects the inside". It is very important to be honest about these belief systems and thereby be realistic rather than using this exercise to compensate for a sense of lack. Use this exercise for spiritual prosperity and psychological contentment so that you are free flowing with the spirit of the universe rather than swimming against the stream of life. As you are open to receiving that which naturally comes with this flow you learn to surrender and give yourself to true love and compassion. This is of course easily achieved when we feel of service to others and it creates a sense of wisdom and freedom that flows into abundance on the material level. Such abundance also requires managing the material level with dignity and generosity and understanding that love is eternal and has no limitations.

STEP ONE

ACKNOWLEDGE THAT WE NO LONGER HAVE SPACE FOR POVERTY CONSCIOUSNESS rather open our unconscious thinking to the powerful hope and recognition of change. This doesn't mean escaping from the reality that we are living in but rather acknowledging our thoughts as real and hence an amazing step that prepares us to get ready to think differently. So this first step would be to change such thinking by perhaps visualising or internally experiencing that this lack is simply a thought, an energy form, and can with practise be replaced with thoughts that better serve you, your family and your community.

STEP TWO

AFFIRM OUR POSITIVE THOUGHTS IN A PRACTICAL SENSE WITH POSITIVE ACTIONS not simply to ourselves but also to our family, our friends and our community. Affirming to ourselves that we are rich, that we are good at everything, that we are physically perfect, that we are intelligent and that we are always reaching our goal, consciously re-writes our thoughts. Once we do this, things begin to take care of themselves so that everything becomes more positive.

STEP THREE

ACT OUT THESE NEW POSITIVE PERSONAL THOUGHTS TO CREATE AN ABUNDANCE beyond the positive focus and energising it so that it grows exponentially - you deserve the best and the abundance keeps growing. Focus upon the growth and the growing rather than the lack.

STEP FOUR

KEEP WATCH ON OUR THOUGHTS so that we do not sabotage our growth. Perhaps we begin to feel uncomfortable in what we are not used to, that which is new and unknown from previous experiences but stay positive. It is important for you to know that by constantly giving power to something on a mental level whether this be conscious or unconscious that miracles happen.

You will be surprised how often we think about ourselves in a negative sense and how easy it is to empower oneself simply with different thoughts.

It is always easier to recognise and relate to an old pattern which has become a habit but understand that the joy of relating to the flow of who you are carries you to a sense of real abundance that is much more powerful. As someone remarked, "old habits die hard".

***

In relation to money we all need to have a relationship with this physical/material aspect because money is everywhere. It dominates our attitudes and cultural sense of who we are whether we believe it to be important or not.

Many of us believe money is the root of all evil but really it is what money does rather than money itself that creates the negative circle of desire. Perhaps it is better said that it is the lust after money that is the root of all evil and as there is no evil it is perhaps better said that it is the lust after money that is the root of all the confusion that we face in today's world and the suffering that it creates in individuals.

When we desire money to fulfil needs then we forget that these needs can more easily be fulfilled by trust, love and sharing rather than spitefully keeping large amounts of money/material wealth in our pocket.

If we use the material to evolve in a more balanced way we realise that money is just another aspect of the energy that we are made of, made visible in a form that we can more easily relate to. Our energy takes on many forms like love, compassion and well-being in this physical world. If money becomes an extension of this then it can be another form of abundance.

It is not bad to have more love or more time or more space or more resources that help us to experience ourselves in a more beautiful way and that help us to be freely abundant. Enjoy the gifts of nature such as good health, pure air, sunshine and the amazing beauties that are free for everyone to experience.

As we free ourselves, we free our thoughts to occupy a new space and notice things that seem invisible to others and by ignoring what once got in the way of such beauty we can focus on the beauty itself.

<u>A lack of wealth is simply an opportunity in disguise.</u>

Financial barriers can pave your road to success but only if you believe and trust yourself to walk on this road by being helpful to others and thus creating more abundance in the energy field that is around you and the sense of who you are.

If you focus on manifesting money alone this limits the real abundance that the universe can provide for you. If you look for personal quantities to put into your pocket then you miss out on the abundant universal quantities that are there to be shared as they will not fit into your pocket. This is one of the greatest gifts that you can acknowledge.

When you acknowledge this you will attract others who can and will help you reach your goals as you help them reach theirs.

<u>Being of service is the secret to success.</u>

You get what you want from life by helping others get what they want. By distributing and providing a wonderful product such as Theriaca Elixir that is a powerful antidote to the negative stresses, environmental pollutions and energy imbalances faced by many of us today you exchange abundance with others which then becomes manifest not only in appreciation and betterment of your fellow beings but also in a material sense and you manifest one of the most beautiful laws of nature - those who serve most get most.

Just look around you and see that highly successful businesses are often those that offer a superior, helpful product that creates deep satisfaction and hence people enjoy and are willing to pay or exchange their abundance for these products.

If you take this opportunity as a path with a desire to serve others by helping them to reach optimum health rather than focus on the money, then this amazing law creates abundance without effort. The motivation for many will often be just money but for real success the motivation has to be to love what you are doing, to believe in what you are doing and to want to share what you are doing with the world.

This is very logical. If love is the most powerful force in the universe then it must be strongly linked with all aspects of who you are including financial abundance.

Theriaca Elixir is such a powerful and beneficial healing agent that in itself, this service is more than satisfying once we receive the positive feedback from the people that we get to know on this wonderful journey. It is very important that we go beyond our fears and be of service rather than focus simply on the money aspect of selling a product. Theriaca Elixir was created to help humanity and as we do this, our finances will reflect our service.

If your goal is love then money will flow like water.

If you have followed the above steps then the greatest block to manifesting such levels of financial abundance will no longer be a hindrance. You will no longer be afraid of being free and sharing your depth with others. You will no longer be afraid of the world you live in and being part of it in a more abundant way. The energy field will no longer magnify any shortcomings that you have believed in. You will magnify your strength as you become more generous to yourself and to others.

You will share in the joy and well-being that you and this wonderful opportunity create for yourself, friends, family, colleagues and people that you meet in a world full of potential and abundance.

One distributor mentioned that it was very helpful for them to read the notes on financial abundance every night prior to sleeping so that they could fall asleep meditating upon the profound words and how they transform their old belief systems and enhance their wonderful journey.

IX. HOW TO PURCHASE THERIACA ELIXIR

To purchase Theriaca Elixir and to understand our unique distribution system and incentives, please visit www.TheriacaElixir.org and read the information provided online. You will also find the list of all our distributors from whom you may purchase Theriaca Elixir. If you have any further questions or need clarifications, please consult the FAQ and in case you are still needing explanations, contact us via e-mail.

Here is what one of our enthusiastic distributors expressed:

"I would like to tell you that I became a distributor of your magic potion, your elixir for longevity, your nectar of life and the most incredible thing is that the formula is given to us by mother nature, the feminine portion of the Divine!

Thanks to your sensibility, magic, alchemy and illumination, you were able to utilise your accumulated wisdom allied with the energy of the Divine and we are the fortunate users!

Thank you!"

A.M. - Portugal

X. RESOURCES

Theriaca Elixir can play a vital role as an antidote to our modern lifestyles, environmental pollution, stresses and imbalances of energy. Many ancient cultures drank healing herbal teas knowing that the adaptogenic, cleansing and rejuvenating tonic ingredients were vital for good health. Rediscover this ancient healing form and empower body, mind and spirit.

www.TheriacaElixir.org

After living for several years in a Zen Buddhist monastery, Tony Samara ventured to the jungles of South America - to the Amazon and to the Andes - where he lived and studied among a community of Shamans. After many years he was initiated in the sacred healing ways of these ancient peoples and left South America to teach and share this deep wisdom with the world.

www.TonySamara.org

We live in such a beautiful world! We invite you to visit the links we recommend on the pages of this website in order to realise just how lucky we are to be alive on the planet at this time and realise the freedom that you have for making a conscious choice that will make a difference.

www.OurBeautifulWorld.org

All of the products at Heart Herbs are powerful and vital healing tools for bringing health and well-being into everyone's daily life. By working with the harmony and cooperation of nature we have created balanced tonics, elixirs, wonderfoods and innovative cleansing products which are at the leading edge of botanical formulations.

www.HeartHerbs.eu

XI. ENVIRONMENTAL AWARENESS, PLANET EARTH PRESERVATION AND ETHICAL & ECOLOGICAL LIVING

Tony Samara was very particular that Theriaca Elixir's container would be totally ecological using non-toxic inks, recycled paper, etc. This container can be reutilised to store grains, cookies, nuts, teas etc. and since it is a food grade material, it contains no chemicals which would be hazardous to human health.

Tony Samara's vision about Environmental Awareness, Planet Earth Preservation and Ethical and Ecological Living lead to the creation of "Our Beautiful World" that expresses in a very simple and direct way many possibilities that make our living more conscious in this planet. Please read the inspiring and enlightening text below taken from Our Beautiful World's website.

"Dear friends,

We live in such a beautiful world!

And beyond words our actions and practical manifestations of ethical living can speak louder to preserve our beautiful world in many more ways than ever before.

The impact of your actions will be very difficult to measure but for sure will make a big difference to you, to your family, to your environment, to your community and hopefully to the world we are living in.

We invite you to visit the links we recommend on the pages of www.OurBeautifulWorld.org in order to realise just how lucky we are to be alive on the planet at this time and realise the freedom that you have for making a conscious choice that will make a difference.

This personal action not only improves your situation but makes a big difference to everyone and creates a more caring culture and a new paradigm for humanity to live by.

It is clear that environmental and social aspects of our lifestyle are being taken seriously. There is a growing awareness of individuals who know that it is possible to increase our positive impact through little and not so little steps that reach far further than we may think.

Help to save the dwindling rainforests of the world by contributing to the Samara Foundation Forest Project and become a guardian of a piece of the precious rainforest in Costa Rica.

Consider building an ecological home.

By eating healthy, organic foods you become part of the solution for global warming.

Read books that are inspiring and uplifting and which teach us about life.

Allow yourself to experience health and well-being.

Teach your children that nature and all its bountiful mysteries is the best teacher and share the treasures of mother earth with the small people who are part of your life.

Drink teas renowned for their healing properties of longevity and well-being.

Holiday in pristine locations and reap the benefits of the healing qualities found there.

Assist the planet and global warming by switching to green solutions for your technological requirements.

And most importantly love yourself, love each other and love the world.

We will be constantly updating our links on all pages of www.OurBeautifulWorld.org and look forward to hearing your feedback.

Unite with us as we create a world worthy for our children and our children's children to live upon.

Love

Our Beautiful World

www.OurBeautifulWorld.org